LEAVING LEGACY
LASTING LEADERSHIP THAT
MAKES A DIFFERENCE

Bruce Williamson

DEDICATION

To my wonderful wife who is the best example of legacy leadership where it matters most — at home and in the community.

CONTENTS

ACKNOWLEDGMENTS

I want to thank the legacy leaders who apprenticed me — Mark, Richard, Neil, David, Sue, Paul, Jon, Kim, Donna. Legacy leaders who inspired me with their boldness – Dr. Bill, Tricia, David, Andy, Chris, Camilla, Debbie, Alex, Samantha, Rodrigo, Pete, Spencer, Bjoern. Legacy leaders who took a chance on me — Rosalind, Jai, Robert. Legacy leaders who cultivated culture-as-a-competitive-advantage — Jeff, Ted, Jen, Jim, Mike, Hoss, CJ, Kim, Nicky, Claire, Ines, Carrie, David, Dal, Juliana, Bryan. I want to especially thank Clay and Mike for their encouragement, contributing keen ideas and role modeling legacy leadership for more than a decade. To our Father – every perfect gift comes from You.

Introduction

I've seen too many leaders walk out the door, or get kicked out the door, from teams and organizations with only a half-hearted goodbye. I've watched too many people pack up their things in boxes and briefcases leaving behind drawers and hard drives full of their work only to leave with a few handshakes then evaporate without a whisper of them again. I've witnessed leaders pour themselves into their work — countless hours rallying us to deliver the results, hit the numbers, land the big deals, nail the deadlines — only to get replaced by someone else with practically the same robotic message, with the same results-at-all-cost idolatry. I've seen too many employees squander too many years stuck, under-developed, under-utilized, because their manager was too busy to do the hard work of developing them.

I've also seen leaders palpably missed not because the rest of us had to cover for them, but because they meant something to us. They left with hugs, not just hand-waves. The people they groomed grew from acorns to oak trees; I could see them over time thrive among their peers, tackle the most recalcitrant problems with zeal, eventually be counted among the most respected leaders that others wanted to work for. People clamored to get on their teams. I was, we were, better because of them.

I wanted to know why leaders can grow up in an organization, be trained in exactly the same way, follow similar career paths, yet some are easily forgotten, others are the brunt of jokes and a rare few propel us long after they leave — their stories flow across teams popping up in conference rooms, one-on-one meetings, or in the most trying of circumstances. What started for me early in my career as a few curious interviews to extract life lessons from soon-to-be-retirees became a passionate pursuit. I have been studying leaders for decades. I started taking notes on positive leaders who shaped teams and organizations for years long after they left; their impact seen in bold paradigm shifts, strategic moves and a long lineage of next generation leaders apprenticed by them. I started taking notes on negative leaders who left empty-hearted and their teams empty-handed. Those hand-written notes strewn over years were jig-saw puzzle pieces that became connected with this project.

Legacy leadership isn't standing out for being different, but making a difference in someone's life, in the fabric of your company, in your community and causes that make you swell with emotion. Legacy isn't reserved for senior leaders, but it is available for all of us. Who is better because of you? Not what...who? People will get dozens of good-enough bosses and co-workers, but legacy leaders shape us differently. They leave a positive impact on everyone they touch.

A leader's legacy is not only about growing business profits and returns. It's also about the imprint a leader has on the people and the organization. We all leave something behind; every leader leaves some kind of legacy — negative, neutral (forgotten) or positive. Your legacy isn't just on when you want it to be. Legacy is always imprinting, always projecting, always molding, always shaping lives around us. Pre-decide your legacy or it will be decided for you. Legacy is formed from intentional moments — some are tiny, hidden interactions and clandestine choices while others are signature, defining, formative. These moments can be crafted, written into epic stories not by passively waiting, but by proactively creating them. We will write those moments together in this book.

Fulfillment at work is more nuanced then simply the pride of achieving target after target, milestone after milestone, year after year. It is possible to be at the top of the pile in our field of achievement and at the bottom of life in professional fulfillment. What if your professional life had purpose? Not just for you but for many. What if your life at work mattered – not because of a role in an org chart, but really mattered to the people you work with? What if you created the conditions, the resolute mindset, the imperishable values for people, for teams to flourish long after you are gone?

This book is meant to challenge you to intentionally go for positive legacy. Anything less is not satisfying to you as a leader and you'll be missing one of the greatest opportunities a leader has in professional life — to make those around you better, more productive and feeling like what they do is lasting, meaningful and makes a difference. This book will help you to see the core tenants of legacy development — The ABC'S of Legacy Leadership — and you will also begin writing your essential legacy stories.

The story examples in the book span "corporate" messages and deeply personal stories inspired by listening to legacy leaders (some imperfectly paraphrased and some verbatim). It's easy to dismiss anonymous personal stories as misplaced in a book about leadership development. Suspend your judgement. As you will see, authenticity, vulnerability and connection are core drivers of legacy formation. Your humanness matters immensely in legacy formation.

Through personal reflection and exercises (Legacy Story Starters), you will craft your personal legacy development plan. I suggest reading the book in short spurts vs. sprinting through it. When you reach Legacy Story Starters asking you to ponder some tough questions, pause. Ideas will spring to mind. You will contemplate how you are showing up. You will begin forming your essential stories. Write down your unrefined thoughts in a journal or use the blank pages at the back of this book (Create Your Story). Equally helpful would be to go through the book with others — your team, a mentor or peer — to share ideas and ideals, hold a mirror up to each other, and hold each other accountable.

Enjoy the journey of discovering your legacy leadership.

1 LEADING WITH LEGACY IN MIND

In that moment when teams, projects, or people inevitably get stuck, that turning point of giving up or getting going…what will you say? In that moment, when your team needs to trust you or trust the past, when conviction is what you need from your team, but anxiety is what they feel…what will you say? In that moment when values are on the line, when it's more convenient to concede your principles then suffer…what will you do? In that moment when customers are departing and your profits are as well, when you don't have enough cash, when the livelihood of your employees is in your hands…what will you do? In that moment when the storms of crisis come rolling in, when competitors are crushing you, when your team looks to you for preparedness, for cover, for courage…what will you say? In that moment when they meet you for the first time, around swirling stories about your past, when reciting your CV seems inadequate, when they are looking to confirm the false rumors…what will you say? In that moment when three leaders have been herded through the department in five years, when a crisis of confidence looms large over disenfranchised employees…what will you say? In that coaching moment when a setback has crushed your mentee, when she has become dismayed, when he has become cheerless…what will you say? In that defining moment, facing the giant — something deeply personal or professionally colossal — when your team has the choice to walk away or stand firm, to lean in or hang back, to heed the heroic call or neglect it…what will you say to embolden them?

And then, when it's all said and done, when you leave the people and work that you love, what will they say about you? Long after you are gone, long after your directives are replaced by someone else's, long after your dashboards and decks are dusty, what stories will they carry in their pocket and pull out just when they need them the most? What stories will be told about you — around a bar or around a conference table, to new hires around a coffee machine or even with their families around the kitchen table?

A Purposeful Life Now Not Later

What if your professional life had purpose? Not just for you but for many. What if your life at work mattered — not because of your place in an org chart, but really mattered to the people you work with? Not because of your irreplaceable skills or your cleverness or your ability to deliver no matter what. But because you made a difference, however great or however small, to people — customers, co-workers, employees, mentees, leaders. What if you created the conditions, the resolute mindset, the imperishable values for people and teams to flourish long after you are gone? What if you imprinted something in the people you work with that was deeply meaningful? What if you were the first to reveal something truly authentic about yourself that broke barriers, wiped away facades and brought your coworkers closer? What if your vulnerability in admitting a mistake stopped others from burying theirs? What if you marked your coworkers with words that they could carry long into their working years, when one-day they will lead and maybe one-day you will follow them? What if you inspired others to carry on the great unfinished work for the company, the profession, the movement you so passionately care about? What if they picked up where you left off? As one worker said, "A legacy is created when your work causes your company to operate differently for years after you leave."

Legacy is a yearning that doesn't stop simply when you enter the doors of your workplace. We all have pleas for meaning even at work. Maybe most at work. If you are going to spend eight to twelve hours a day away from your family, from your dear friends, from your partner than it should count for something. Our tendency is to pass our lessons to others after our working lives settle down. Isn't that an empty promise we tell ourselves every year – "Once I have a little time, then I'll ...?" What if the people we lead need our wisdom now, not when it's perfectly convenient for *us* to share it? Our influence has worth throughout different seasons of *their* lives, throughout *their* varied circumstances — not just when we have thick margins in *our* lives. When workers are asked to define legacy, it's rarely defined at the end of someone's career, but rather *during* a career — shaping organizational culture in the moment such that it endures beyond your tenure. Your stories are a wellspring that your organization and your people are thirsty for. Maybe not today, but eventually. If we wait too long, we will literally miss a once-in-a-lifestage chance to influence them.

Can you really prepare your bright high potential employee to place others first, to put others on the pedestal when they so desperately desire center stage? Surely. Can you inspire your team to pick up the pieces of brokenness — failed launches, devastating reorganizations, losing market share — and encourage them to start moving again? Yes. Can you set a good example when you always haven't been? Certainly. Can you teach lessons when you are still learning? Absolutely. Can you encourage team members to stay the course, to follow the plan and believe wholly in the mission when everything around them seems to be unraveling? Indeed. Can you give them hope, infuse joy in their long days, and instill a deep connection among team members even where there are contrasting styles and stark differences? Yes.

We Can All be Legends
Few see themselves as useful beyond their title or profession,

and that is tragic. Legends are prominent around us; we're looking in the wrong places. Rarely are legends larger-than-life heroes. They are unassuming leaders. They are coworkers, service personnel and line workers. They are everyday people in our lives doing the impossible. Everyone has the potential to be someone's role model. Everyone has the potential to prop up others' strengths, build their capability, encourage their growth.

Legacy isn't standing out for being different, but making a difference: in someone's life, in the fabric of your company's business, in your community and causes that make you swell with emotion. Legacy isn't reserved to "management" or "corporate" or "bosses." Legacy isn't the exclusive purview of senior leaders. Legacy is for all of us. Where legacy is formed, someone made a leadership decision: to break a rule, to take a chance on someone, to fight rather than flee, to stand up and stand alone, to be a voice, to invest in someone. The ability to imprint the best of you into the lives of co-workers, into the fabric of your organization, is available to everyone — from the remarkably optimistic administrator to the ebullient technician to the demanding team leader who brings out your giftedness. In fact, in my research, I've found ample evidence that positive legacy is readily created by co-workers, peers, managers and supervisors, not just executives. Legacy at work is available to all of us, and it can be one of the most fulfilling and meaningful outcomes of your work life.

How do you make meaning from work? University of Pennsylvania Wharton professor Adam Grant found in his research that what motivates employees is "doing what affects the well-being of others" and to "see or meet people affected by their work." What if we abandoned the cultural definition of success and we instead oriented toward a different goal — one that uses a different yardstick, a yardstick of not just nailing objectives, crashing timelines and amassing zeroes in our bank accounts. Maybe we need to reframe our perspective. Maybe fulfillment at work is more nuanced than simply the pride of achieving target after target, project after project, milestone after milestone, year after year.

What will you leave that is noble? Noble doesn't always mean heroic, overcoming against death-defying odds, endangering our life for others, slaying dragons. A grand nobility resides in each of us that forges meaning in our lives and enriches the lives of others. There are scores of people who dedicate time, care and effort in their ordinary lives to create something extraordinary for their co-workers, their organizations, and their communities. They intentionally apprentice others, not with an occasional "one-on-one meeting" where the priority is checking on progress, but with the intent of imparting wisdom, growing their mentees' potential, coaching them to perform to their fullest, and bringing out the best in them.

Are you preparing them — not with statements but with stories, real stories, your stories, their stories — to be resilient, to be bold, to be curious, to be gritty, to be authentic? Are you raising their performance, their engagement, their passionate pursuit for self-growth? Are you imprinting your bold ideas and battle-tested lessons to those around you?

Who is better because of you? Not what — who? Will someone be thankful for you, grateful for your mentorship, appreciative of your guidance amid tough choices? Because of you, will they be a little more courageous, a little more strategic, a little better listener, a little more gritty, a little more balanced between work and home, a little more tenacious, a little more human?

Will you leave them a well when life at work inevitably leaves them a little thirsty? What are the things they still need to learn from you? How will you refresh them?

Will you leave them with a map and compass when they inevitably get a little lost in life? What path will they take? Because they won't stand still. They will keep moving, sometimes along the trails you have marked for them and sometimes with only their trusted instincts to go by. Your successors can either get directions from you – their leader, their mentor — or someone else, sometimes a stranger.

The Significance of Stories

Deep down everyone wants to be proud of their life stories. But stories only survive if they are passed on and picked up by others. What stories do you want told? What do you want to be remembered for? What stories would you like to be passed on to those around you, behind you, in front of you? What stories will others tell when you leave?

The stories told about us can be positive, negative or empty. The stories repeated across teams can be chock full of wisdom, epithets of encouragement, nourishment just when we need it. Or, those stories can be dry vessels, empty, useless. Worse, stories can be full of vinegar souring cheerful employees or venom poisoning even the most promising talent. Why do we talk positively about some people when they leave? Why do we still tell their heroic stories? Why have their stories become our stories? Why have they become like war heroes full of honor and valor, preparing an army of next generation leaders? Why do we notice their mark, palpably miss their presence while others simply depart sometimes with only a half-hearted goodbye or as the brunt of jokes?

Choose your legacy or it will be chosen for you. If you don't decide in advance what stories you want told — not *about you* like gossip, but *from you* —then it will be decided for you. You can be intentional about stories being legacy*ful* — positive, encouraging, lasting, fulfilling, meaningful. Or your stories can be legacy*less* — self-serving, forgotten, hollow, useless. People certainly don't become legacy*less* intentionally. No one intends to have their work simply evaporate when they leave. What our organizations and teams crave isn't a pleasant work life, but meaningful one. What if you created the conditions for great stories to be written — the team culture, the compelling vision, the bold plan, the motivating movement for people to passionately pursue something difference-making, a reason to get up in the morning beyond the alarm clock?

Small and Big Moments Matter

Legacy is always imprinting, always projecting, always molding, always shaping lives around us.

Legacy is formed from moments. Some of those moments are tiny, hidden interactions and clandestine choices while others are signature, defining, shaping. Moments are the DNA of stories. Seemingly tiny interactions we take for granted every day accumulate to strengthen our relationships like countless drops of water filling a vessel. Our professional lives are made up of these seemingly inconsequential moments, but those moments build habits, mold values, teach lessons, establish behaviors, write stories. Or they can dilute values, fracture relationships, destroy credibility, embitter jobs, crush talent. Our legacy is determined moment to moment to moment.

Defining moments are punctuating events or circumstances that are often thrust upon us; the experience and outcomes become embedded in our personal narrative. These defining moments are ripe for legacy stories. Lose their significance in the moment, and, at best you lose a meaningful opportunity; at worst you derail projects and disengage people.

When we are conscious of building legacy, we become deeply intentional. Creating, not wasting moments. Creating the conditions that deliver results and the enduring experiences that positively mark people and the organization. When we are conscious of building legacy, we see defining moments with keen foresight — seeing their potential to build a meaningful story — so we ask, "What story do I want told?" Behaviors, decisions, attitudes that follow are likely to be legacy*ful* not legacy*less*.

Working for Lasting Value

What am I doing here? *Here* usually isn't a physical place. Rather, it's something different for each of us — a lifestyle, a career, an emotional state, an attitude toward work, coworkers, your boss. Some will work their entire lives coaching an army of passionate professionals who are principled, determined and committed to meaningful work that matters. Others will work their entire lives to be rich at last, only to realize they have worked for absolutely nothing that lasts. When we try to satisfy the elusive three P's of Prosperity — Possessions, Position and Power – over the three P's of Posterity — Purpose, Principles, Priorities, we end up momentarily satisfied, but eventually empty and continuously searching. Real meaning in professional life isn't simply personal gain. Ask any retiree.

We often don't realize just how far we have drifted from the work that used to make us happy, the easy decisions that were non-negotiable even at the expense of personal profit, the collaboration among peers without any rivalry or envy. Things won't change unless we do. Running faster won't help. We need to get off the treadmill of success and onto the trek of building significance through legacy building. We are running so fast that we bump into everyday situations that can be defining moments for us, but we are too busy, too tired, too exhausted to recognize their significance.

Do something that counts. Not something that counts by society's definition, but by your own. Doing the work you are called to do rather than the work you just do for prestige or a paycheck. What we are searching for in our professional lives — the potential to be part of something bigger than ourselves, to be procreative with our ideas, to grow others — is not out there in the corporate world unveiled magically with the next promotion. It is here inside us. It's been inside you all along. Legacy building is the fulfillment we are searching for. Legacy leading is the climb of our lives.

Who, when they look back, will say that you are one of the greatest leaders they have worked with? Why you?

Are you a Legacy Leader?

Legacy leaders are guardians of our hearts. They invested in us, mentored us, walked beside us, before us, behind us. They picked us up off the ground. They took a chance on us. If you want to be a legacy leader, you need to stop asking, "What do I need?" Rather, ask, "What do I have and will give in service for others?" We all have something to give: gifts, convictions, characteristic traits, signature stories. The reward for legacy work is not what you get out of it, but what you become from it.

If social scientists have taught us anything, it is that people need role models; they need heroes. They need life-tested wisdom, the wisdom that can't come from books or conferences, but can only come when forged through experiences. They need someone to look up to. They need to believe in strengths over weaknesses. They want proof that hard work and practice lead to achievement. They need hope in peaks after valleys, triumph after setbacks, regrowth after fire. They need to see adversity as a gift because meaning is forged in adversity. Because character is forged in adversity. Because connection is forged in adversity. They want to come up taller.

What kind of man or woman does it take to make a permanent impact in an ailing organization, in teams thirsty for purpose, in emerging leaders hungry for growth? In our culture it seems like everything nailed down is coming loose. Stalwart values are being chipped away. Tied knots are fraying. Brittle relationships are nearing fracture. Schedules are full but empty of fulfillment. People are looking for the glue. Where is the glue? Can it be in the stories legacy leaders tell?

Few of us can recall the objectives and goals that defined our lives for twelve-month sprints in our work lives. *Push for 20. Deliver 102. Make the numbers. Let's get to 37.5.* You know what I mean — the words and numbers that spanned banners, hammered into your monthly meetings, maybe even discussed at the dinner table. Remember how important they were at the time? With cultish fervor, they often defined your salary increases, your bonuses, your performance reviews. Now can you remember any of them — these words and numbers that defined your work life for twelve months?

Now, recall a moment when someone made a deep impression on you at work, something that marked you, imprinted something deep inside of you. Maybe a story you've never told anyone, or maybe it's one you've told dozens of times. We don't enter work just a few years after high school character-ready for professional life. We don't enter our first management role with anything more than naïve experiences. Some will have a distinct advantage because of legacy leaders. Bold decisions, engaged teams, wise choices, a pipeline of emerging leaders — these don't just happen. Someone's example, someone's experience, someone's story was likely imprinted on you.

I entered leadership in an era that celebrated bravado, brash, authoritative male leaders. I didn't want that to be my style – not as a new leader. But he stood in stark contrast. He refused a designated parking spot, he listened first to everyone in a meeting then spoke, he opened his door to everyone from the machine operators to effervescent newbies and grumpy old timers. He magnetically pulled people with determination, inspiration and hope rather than pushing them with his title, undermining remarks and tacit threats. He didn't just care that I delivered, but he cared about me...as a person. I looked up to him, confided in him, modeled my management style after him, and he shaped me as a leader. He took a chance on me. He saw something in me that I didn't see in myself.

He asked me to trust him, to take a leap into a new career path because he saw something in me that I didn't in myself. And I thrived. It unleashed something passionate in me. He expected greatness from me, and taught me how to expect it from myself and my team. Even when he was sick with an incurable disease that slowly eroded his motor functions, his breathing, his eating, until a certain death — he gave his all. Just weeks before his death, I was faced with a difficult career decision. He wasn't seeing visitors anymore, but I sent a text to his wife. "He wants to see you in 30 minutes," she responded. This shell of a man, physically frail, but hearty in spirit, incomprehensibly joyful to see me, opened his heart with poignant, wise advice – "Believe in yourself like I do in you, and live with no regrets," he breathlessly whispered, "then you'll know what to do."

Even today, more than a decade later, I think of him almost every week, try to emulate him when I mentor young leaders, when I am faced with a tough decision, when the loneliness of leading and self-doubt of crisis creeps in. He cared for me, covered for me, watched out for me. Not in a paternalistic way, but as a mentor. He held an umbrella for me and now I'm holding it for others.

The reward for legacy building is not what you get out of it, but what you become from it. Legacy leadership is about becoming bigger on the inside than the outside. It's an internal transformation. When you look back on your work life in the rearview mirror, will you see a legacy that gives you a sense of deep satisfaction — values in action, an army of change agents, determined teams? It's never too late to carve your initials in the stories of co-workers, leaders, and members of your community. Let's start building your legacy today.

Legacy Story Starters

Who has left a legacy in your life? In your family? At work? In your community? Of the countless people you have intersected with in your life, why them?

What do you want people to say about you when you leave your place of work?

In your current role, what do you want to leave behind that is lasting and meaningful?

When people look back and say that you are one of the greatest leaders they have worked with, what about you will they be remembering?

To get a litmus test of your own legacy leadership, complete the assessment below. Be authentic and objective — humans have an infinite capacity for self-deception. If you are unsure, ask someone who works with you or for you.

LEGACY ASSESSMENT

1. How many people would say that you left something behind that made a meaningful, lasting difference to them as a person, their team or their organization?

Unsure			Several			Many
1	2	3	4	5	6	7

2. How frequently do you spend at least 30 minutes mentoring or coaching others? Not time spent checking on progress, but intentionally portioned time to selflessly develop others.

Rarely			Weekly		More than once a week	
1	2	3	4	5	6	7

3. Do you exercise small acts of rebellious disobedience to the status quo? Do you frame questions in a way that propels thinking and breaks paradigms by setting a bold ambition amid real constraints?

Sometimes			Frequently		Almost Always	
1	2	3	4	5	6	7

4. Do you have a teachable point of view — a clear set of ideas, values, skilled knowledge and experience — that is articulated in simple lessons?

Not really			Sort of		Definitely	
1	2	3	4	5	6	7

5. Are you on the prowl looking for people to take on more responsibility, to teach them new things, stretch them and bring out their hidden talents whether they report to you or not?

Rarely			Sometimes		Quite Often	
1	2	3	4	5	6	7

6. Have you demonstrated you are a catalyst for change, working outside the expected scripts and operating constraints to make change possible for your team and organization?

    Rarely   Sometimes   Quite Often
    1   2   3   4   5   6   7

7. In your last five assignments, have you created a bold, meaningful, inspiring vision for those you work with or for those who work for you?

    Rarely   Occasionally   Almost Always
    1   2   3   4   5   6   7

8. How often do you demonstrate making courageous decisions that require you to stand alone or against-the-grain? When have you 'heeded the call' to make a difficult, unpopular or contentious decision where something big was on the line?

    Rarely   Occasionally   Almost Always
    1   2   3   4   5   6   7

9. How often do you express gratitude or recognition to others without reservation?

    Rarely   Occasionally   Almost Always
    1   2   3   4   5   6   7

10. How often do you share something vulnerable and personal, mistakes and missteps, revealing the real you, not a public persona you want others to see?

    Rarely   Occasionally   Almost Always
    1   2   3   4   5   6   7

11. Do you have a collection of signature stories and how often do you use them to influence and communicate to your mentees, teams, and co-workers?

Rarely   Occasionally   Almost Always
1   2   3   4   5   6   7

12. Are you the kind of leader who sees the greatness in others, how to uniquely coach them to be better and bring out the best in them? Do you stretch them in ways that illuminate hidden gifts and talents?

Rarely   Occasionally   Almost Always
1   2   3   4   5   6   7

13. Do you set high expectations for yourself and everyone around you? Are you a leader known to be tough and exacting when the stakes are high? Do you challenge not to find fault, but to advance the thinking? Are you a leader who makes those around you more capable?

Unlikely   Not sure   Absolutely
1   2   3   4   5   6   7

14. When you look at your organization, do you see your unique leadership DNA in the people you work alongside? Are you preparing your mentees and co-workers to just deliver results or be the next generation of leaders?

Unlikely   Occasionally   Absolutely
1   2   3   4   5   6   7

15. Who, when they look back, will say that you took a chance on them?

No one   Several   Many
1   2   3   4   5   6   7

16. When the stakes are high have you demonstrated that you can turn fear into faith? Do you express contagious positivity and hope? Have your mentees and teams demonstrated resilience amid setbacks and tense circumstances?

Rarely			Occasionally		Quite often	
1	2	3	4	5	6	7

17. Do you boldly lean into the most recalcitrant problems even if it's not your responsibility? Do you choose to be the initiator, the encourager, the person who puts her hand up first, the person who leads the revolution?

Rarely			Occasionally		Definitely	
1	2	3	4	5	6	7

18. Do you actively create a culture of "in it together," constructive conflict and respectful debate, uncompromising standards and mutual accountability?

Not sure		Probably			Definitely	
1	2	3	4	5	6	7

Add up your answers _____

<80:   You are poised to build the foundations of legacy. Let's get intentional and focused.

81-100:   You are already on the path toward developing a legacy. Let's refine and amplify.

>100:   Impressive legacy building skills. Let's multiply your influence by coaching others.

2   THE ABC'S OF LEGACY LEADERSHIP

My research into legacy at work included quantitative surveys, biographical reviews, academic studies and in-depth interviews with dozens of leaders and workers across generations. Invariably, nearly every respondent's first example of legacy was a negative one. With examples seared into their work experience, it was as if the hurt, the frustration, the bitterness needed an outlet. "Can you believe, (s)he..." followed by some story of selfishness, bullying or simply poor management. One respondent said, "He made work seem like work. He demotivated those around him so it was drudgery. He made an 8-hour day seem like a 12-hour day. I was dead on Mondays and lived for Fridays." Negative legacy is poisonous — to careers, to identities, and, to my surprise, to others' behaviors and attitudes. Some interviewees could see how they'd slowly, subtly changed at work and at home because of a toxic leader. One worker said, "I could see the cancer of negativity, criticism and back-handed comments spread across the organization. It never existed before he showed up, but now it spread and it felt awful. I started behaving in ways that I wasn't proud of, but felt like I needed to for survival."

If negative legacy leaders are a poison then positive legacy leaders are the elixir, catapulting capabilities, confidence, and careers. Positive legacy leaders hold a special honor and devotion. Stories about them are continually referenced; respondents see how these leaders shaped their lives and their organization. One worker said, "They unequivocally support their team. They drive cultural shifts and break down barriers to change that benefit the organization. They are willing to take risks when it comes to moving themselves and their people forward." People are better, in as many forms as you can imagine from values and character traits to results and bold decisions, because of legacy leaders. Another worker said, "They leave people and an organization better than when they first encountered them. It's about investing in others and going the extra mile to help make others find their strengths, get the most out of their gifts and talents and be better at what they do."

More than one hundred workers provided insight into the core elements of legacy including rating their current and past leaders for positive, negative or neutral legacy. Despite different industries, locations, unique backgrounds and levels in their organizations, the core factors of leaving a legacy in organizations were quite consistent and revealing. Just as fascinating were the compelling benefits to employees and team mates of legacy leaders. You'll see the results later in this chapter.

I studied retirees with passion. After all, if there were a cluster of people who had a sweeping, candid perspective on what mattered and what didn't in work life, what they regretted and what they cherished, it would be retirees. After interviewing dozens of retirees and those close to retirement about late/post work life, I got a frank, honest and clear sense of their pride and self-satisfaction, their regrets and discontentment stemming from deep introspection. There wasn't wallowing in sadness; there wasn't bitterness. But in their soul-searching and self-reflection, there were straightforward lessons. If they could do it all over again, they might do some things differently — this I wanted to know. They offered wise guidance those they mentor – children and grandchildren, former employees and college students, rising executives and close colleagues.

It's easy to pass off lessons from retirees as far too distant for those early in their career or as the sappy purview of older generations. But it's dangerous to assume we can't learn from the counsel of generations before us. Certainly the workforce has changed. But human nature has and will forever remain the same. Their lessons are highly relevant because they underscore an elusive insight often missed in the jargon of the workplace — how human we really are at work. All of us, regardless of age, education, and income, crave to have our fundamental, basic human needs met: care and connection with others, growth and competence, control and independence, achievement and recognition, contribution and self-expression. Maybe it's not a generational thing but a life experience thing. What if their hindsight became our foresight? What if we could avoid the late-stage regrets and get more intentional about the rewards? Could life at work be more fulfilling? Below are narratives, pieced-together quotes and paraphrases from interviews with retirees – it's their words. Listen to the wise words of shop keepers to senior executives. Hear from those who have the work experience of two to four decades, their regrets and their rewards.

Regrets of the Retired

Improper priorities and seeking the wrong applause. *I worked so hard at the expense of my family. I waited too long for the right time to shift the work-family balance. I found myself year after year with the same empty refrain — one more year. Surely they can wait one more year. Until they stopped believing me and then they stopped waiting.*

But when I walked out that door – as many times as I thought they just couldn't do it without me – my company simply moved on without me. I realized too late that I was perfectly replaceable at work.

In my undisciplined pursuit of more — more money, more titles, more recognition — I marginalized the few things that really mattered — my family, friends and faith.

I was always thinking about what was next and unintentionally found myself waiting for the payoff that would keep me satisfied. But it never happened. *"Suffer now, happiness later,"* I'd tell myself. Money kept me in the wrong job too long. I really enjoyed coaching people, but I never made it a priority because it never seemed to matter in terms of my performance review.

Inauthentic Self. *I wish I'd had the courage to be true to my gifts instead of pleasing others...being sort of dictated by the expectations of others. It seemed like someone else was prioritizing my life, not intentionally, but I didn't feel like I had control of my work...I didn't speak up enough to choose the things I really wanted to learn or work on.*

I worried I wasn't qualified or I couldn't measure up so I over-emphasized fixing my weaknesses over using my strengths. I worried too much of what others thought of me and forfeited my freedom to be myself, doing the work I was asked to do vs. what I felt I was really good at, the work that brought me happiness. I needed to stop thinking about pleasing people...I needed to let go of the person others wanted me to be and start being myself.

The culture started to change me. I could see it, my wife could see it, but I couldn't let go....I started becoming bitter, my nasty attitude was uncharacteristic...my identity seemed to change.

Treadmill of Busyness over Boldness and Bravery. *I wish I'd faced challenges more instead of waiting for others to do it. I was afraid to fail and it paralyzed me...It didn't really hurt my career, but looking back it feels a bit unfulfilled. I was cautious and not very daring; I was playing it safe and used the excuse of being too busy to really dig in and help fix problems that we all could see, but none of us were specifically responsible for.*

I spent years preparing, waiting to get that promotion. Then I found myself making conservative decisions to protect my career vs. making bolder decisions that could have been risky for me but better for the business. I felt like I had nowhere to go but down; I'd worry about taking risks. When my status was on the line (which it never really was, but I felt that way), I'd act too conservatively, protecting my reputation.

Sure, I was busy, but I always prioritized the urgent over the important so I rarely really felt like I created anything truly valuable.

Those targets which were burned in my brain one year were soon forgotten the next. I spent too much of my time putting my career needs first and letting those I was responsible for languish.

Month after month, I worked really hard but never really felt like I moved the needle or accomplished anything that seemed to matter. "Next time I will" I'd tell myself...but some opportunities never came around again.

Poor victim role. I spent too much time acting like the victim, waiting for "management" to fix the problem instead of enlisting the support of others and doing it myself. I seemed to spend more time whining than getting in and getting the work done.

I lacked the ambition to make change...I was just tired of all the politics, too beaten down to do something big in that company even though I knew what needed to be done. I kept blaming resources, processes and other people rather than facing reality and my responsibility.

I was so cynical, complaining that management wasn't making any changes, but then I complained when change happened. I destroyed any hope for my team, and we resisted trying anything new. I kept waiting for management to come in and fix the problems that I saw but never tried to solve...sometimes I just gave up too easily.

Rewards of the Retired

People are the Big Payoff. In those last few weeks, those last few days of working, what surprised me the most was the people. After delivering dozens of big projects, making my numbers year after year, almost none of that mattered. The most unlikely people came to thank me and recalled small little things I'd done that impressed them or helped them. I never knew people even noticed and I honestly couldn't remember some of them, but they could with incredible detail.

I really miss the opportunity to grow others, to see others succeed, to watch them emerge as leaders, to see them apply my bits of advice and learn from my mistakes. One of my proudest moments was seeing someone who worked for me become a leader and thank me for mentoring her. Watching those who worked for me rise up and become leaders, *those that I even worked for later in my life, it made me proud.*

The (often avoided) struggles matter most. *When I tried and failed is when I learned the most about myself. When I was brave was when I felt most alive. I don't know where I would be without them (struggles)...kind of funny how that worked...the struggles I so anxiously avoided are what I remember.*

I don't remember the easy moments — the peace I often wanted — but the tense circumstances that tried me, tested me, made me into a better employee. I found my voice to lead from the messiness of failing, temporarily; I didn't let failure define me. Coming out on the other side of that struggle was the turning point for me. I walked away stronger.

Meaning. *I remember the work that really mattered, the initiatives that weren't just about saving money or making money, because they were important not just to some of us, but to all of us.*

Working on that project made me feel like I was making a difference, and that made me so proud. I remember telling my kids and friends what I was working on with a deep sense of satisfaction.

It didn't feel like work; it felt like something honorable.

Lead small revolutions. *Those times when I fearlessly faced challenges, when no one else thought we could get it to the finish line, when everyone else in the industry didn't think it was possible, we did the impossible. I'm still proud of that years later.*

With practically no resources and just a handful of us, we turned around that business. We took something that was broken and fixed it...like fixing a car with our bare hands.

I remember a stranger coming up to me in the hallway and shaking my hand because he'd heard what we had done, what we had gone through, how important that project was to the rest of the organization. I remember thinking, "This feels good. To think I almost passed it up because I was chicken."

Deep Personal Change. *I'd fallen into a complacency of complaining, criticizing, finger-pointing. A colleague one day told me* *that my attitude was killing her and the team. If I was that unhappy, then leave. That was my turning point. I was determined to stop waiting for the change, waiting for someone to lead the change and instead I took charge. It started with a better attitude. That was the best year of my career.*

I remember the day I decided to stop counting the years to retirement and dig in to make things better. I really enjoyed the work and the people.

My wife of all people told me one day, "You either need to quit or quit complaining because you are miserable and you are being childish."

Appreciation. *One of the greatest days of my working life was when someone said thank you, grateful for the role I had in her life, how I made a deep impression on her professional life.*

I felt so appreciated. Someone stopped by my office during my last week and told me how much I was a role model for him, how much he admired my resolve, my leadership, my dedication, how he had been watching me from a distance for years and tried to act similarly.

I'd thought my decisions and actions were largely invisible until my retirement day, when people stood up and recalled those little moments when I made a difference for them.

What Goes into Leaving a Legacy

Ask workers what they most admired and remembered from leaders and peers in organizations long after they are gone and you'll find surprising congruity. And it's not what you think. It's not delivering on time and on budget; it's not exceeding sales targets; it's not even the thrill of new product launches. It's not the what, but the how. As one worker stated, "The individuals who created a positive legacy were those who were consistently true to themselves personally and professionally and understood their legacy was larger than just themselves. Their integrity, perseverance and above all ability to remain human in interactions across all levels and organizational departments was what transformed them from average to great. These folks were, without realizing it, making more of an impact on others around them by the way they were going about completing the work rather than the success of the work itself. These great leaders knew that by unlocking the potential of their teams and others they ensured that dramatic and positive results would be achieved."

In the legacy survey I conducted, when asked to choose only three ways people can create legacy at work—something left behind that is lasting and meaningful to people and organization—here's what rose to the top:

82% selected *A commitment to mentoring and growing others so they can be better*
54% selected *A passion and perseverance for developing and executing a bold vision/plan*
59% selected *A desire to create a high performance, engaging team/workplace culture*
49% selected *A deep, authentic connection to others*

What wasn't selected as ways of leaving legacy (those receiving less than a 25% as a top 3 choice): character traits, making tough decisions, exceptional managerial skills, charisma and presence, delivering exceptional results, and managing through a crisis. As one respondent stated, "Most people can help the business achieve or exceed their goals. To me, leaving a legacy is all about the way you do it. You need to promote a positive working environment, be honest with team members and push them to be better. Leaving something behind that is more than results."

The Deep and Wide Benefits of Legacy Leaders

According to Gallup, three in four people who voluntarily leave their jobs don't quit their company, they quit their bosses. Just about half of employees do not feel inspired by their leaders. There is a nearly a pandemic level of indifference toward work. Legacy is a human-based yearning — to do something that counts and leave something behind — that doesn't stop simply when you enter the doors of our workplace. We all have a desire for meaning in our lives. Countless men and women reach points in their professional career with eerily similar uncertainties, regrets, and hesitations:

Is this all?

Is this how I want to be remembered?

Is this all I want?

What happened to my passion?

However, the benefits to an organization of leaders who left a positive legacy are impressive. Recalling positive legacy leaders, survey respondents cited the following benefits:

82% agree, *I was more loyal to the team/organization*

85% agree, *I worked harder and was more engaged at work because I felt I was making a difference.*

65% agree, *I grew my leadership skills and abilities.*

78% say, *I am practicing what they role modelled.*

64% agree, *My confidence improved.*

65% agree, *I grew personally.*

45% say, *I used my strengths more.*

43% say, *I improved on a weakness.*

Prevalence of Positive and Negative Legacy Leadership

In the legacy study, workers were asked to contemplate five leaders they have either worked with directly or indirectly (yet close enough to assess). They were asked if each leader created negative legacy for them or their organization, no legacy, some positive legacy or significant positive legacy for them or their organization. Over six hundred leaders were assessed in total. Qualitative explanations provided an additional layer of insight. The results reveal that for these respondents less than one in three leaders left positive legacy — the remaining two of every three leaders left either no legacy or negative legacy.

Negative legacy leaders are surprisingly prominent. A little more than one in five leaders created negative legacy for people and/or their organization. These negative legacy leaders were described with the following phrases:

"Only cared about their results. Trampled teammates in the process"

"...making personal gain more important than organizational objectives. You didn't win or lose as a team."

"Results were achieved but at the cost of the team."

"...arrogance, narcissism, bias, dictatorial, gloryhounds."

"No vision to win and lacking the skill to inspire and bring the team along on the journey."

"Took a don't-rock-the-boat approach as opposed to championing a will to win."

"...inflexible, rigid in thinking and stuck in process over results"

"He never trusted my work, always finding something wrong or to complain about...avoided conflict so there was never a crucial conversation to understand or intently listen."

"Focused on mistakes instead of success. They do not lead people by leveraging their strengths."

"...operated in a setting where every request is urgent, but he did nothing to remove barriers impeding progress...the culture operates under duress."

"Eventually the gap between what he said and what he did got big enough for people to stop listening."

Toxic culture, bullying bosses, incivility, disrespect and intimidation are booming in peer-reviewed research. A Google Scholar search on abusive management from 2008 to 2016 returns more than 5,500 scholarly articles and books; rudeness generates more than 16,000 citations and bullying an amazing nearly 140,000. More than fifty percent of working Americans say they have experienced or witnessed persistent bullying, but less than one percent admit to doing it (Sutton, 2017). One worker said it best: "I'm not sure why, but I've seen it too often — not just here, but in other places too — you need to be bad to achieve something good."

According to a study by psychologist Michelle McQuaid, the majority of Americans are unhappy in the workplace namely due to their bosses. About 70% of respondents say they would be happier and 55% say they would be more successful if they got along better with their supervisor, according to the survey. More than 65% of people would rather have a better boss than a salary increase (Casserly, 2012). Here are some revealing highlights from McQuaid's survey of over 1,000 workers:

-Only 36% of survey respondents say they are happy at their job.

-65% say a better boss would make them happy while 35% would choose a pay raise

-31% of employees polled feel uninspired and unappreciated by their boss.

-Only 38% of those polled describe their boss as "great," with 42% saying their bosses don't work very hard and close to one in five saying their boss has little or no integrity.

-When asked about the impact a bad supervisor could have on their health, 73% of those in their 20s and 30s said their health is at stake.

In the hard-nosed world of business books, Stanford professor Bob Sutton wrote a book on bad corporate behavior — *The Asshole Survival Guide: How to Deal with People Who Treat You Like Dirt.* Sutton says that there are numerous culprits for the spreading rash of workplace dysfunction: hyper-competition in the global economy, overburdened leaders and teams, email, texting, and social media replacing face-to-face conversation and hence stripping away empathy, civility and old-fashioned talking it out. Some executives inexcusably believe that treating people badly is the path to success, worrying that treating people with dignity and with measured calm isn't seen as "tough enough." One worker commented on negative legacy leaders, "They drag dead bodies to try to climb the ladder. No one likes them."

About forty-five percent of people said the leaders they worked with directly or indirectly created no legacy at all. This is empty work fulfillment and empty leadership. Day after day, year after year of time invested in work — away from family, friends and pursuits they deeply care about — only to evaporate from a workplace one day and leave practically nothing but a stapler and an empty chair behind. Tragic. No one plans for this. But without intentionality, its likelihood is real.

Then there are those that carry the honor of positive legacy leaders. Seventeen percent said positive legacy was left for their team or organization. Fourteen percent said significant positive legacy was created for them personally. Legacy leaders generate more loyalty, grow employees more, and elicit dedication because their teams have a deeper sense of satisfaction. People who create positive legacy hold a special place in the hearts of workers. Listen to how people describe what sets them apart.

"She was uncompromising in her values and laser focused on a mission. She motivated and energized me — she made work fun and exciting. Others went out of their way to be around her because she made you feel like you were living out your destiny."

"Boldness, bordering on hubris, to go it alone even with the intense judgement from others. He had an ability to engage and mobilize teams...The picture he painted of the future was the magic elixir."

"A unique mix of ego and altruism to help others succeed—often putting them squarely in the spotlight of criticism — while demanding excellence of themselves and others."

"She shifted the culture. The results were there as well, but they were there because she was able to inspire people to follow her and support her vision."

"Clear vision and know-how to create a sense of purpose, she was authentic with enduring values and she was good at changing culture by rewarding good practices and penalizing bad ones."

"...make tough situations easier keeping a positive and realistic sense of what needs to be done and did it with a smile."

"An uncanny ability to be courageous in the face of what seemed to be perceived as an obstacle, but turned into a lasting opportunity that broke through paradigms that we never knew could be overcome."

"Positive energy, willingness to take on problems that other ignore, stubborn determination to make change, embrace change."

"Stretched me to do my best by setting clear objectives, allowed me to manage my own work and provided honest (both good and bad) feedback on my progress."

"Everyone knows them. They are incredible people. You want to be on their team because you will grow like crazy."

Positive legacy leaders prominently stand-out among us. Rarely are they larger-than-life heroes. They are everyday people in our work and communities — co-workers who challenge the status quo and set a course for change, managers who put their people on stage but take responsibility when problems arise, leaders who place values above profit. A legacy leader never knows where his or her influence stops. Interviewing teams with legacy leaders, you can see small bits of legacy DNA moving from person to person. You can see values transferred, you can see the courage of one bold decision propagating a multiple of different bold decisions. You can see ways of working consistent, principled across diverse individuals. When people transfer, you can see similar fragments of legacy DNA sprout up in other teams. You hear unforgettable stories imprinted and firmly networked across people and teams.

From the legacy survey, you could say that workers have a less than 50:50 chance of getting a leader that creates a positive legacy compared to one that either creates no legacy or negative legacy for them and their organization. Will you be a negative or positive legacy leader others say shaped and molded them *in spite of you* or *because of you*?

The ABC's of Legacy Building Framework

When you ask people what distinguishes legacy leaders from the long line of people they have worked alongside, when you ask what they distinctly remember, when you ask what's salient and remarkable about these people, when you query workers on the few, core elements of legacy generation, there are surprising commonalities. If you want to leave something behind that's meaningful, lasting, significant, then you need to follow the

ABC'S of Legacy Building at Work.

Apprenticing: Mentoring others and stewarding their gifts to grow their potential. Personally investing in coaching, upskilling, developing, encouraging, serving others. Preparing them for their next role. Shining a light on their greatness. Grounding simultaneous life wisdom and professional wisdom. Positively labelling them and helping them overcome derailers. Ask: Who are you preparing and growing with intentionality? What will you imprint on others to accelerates their growth?

Boldness: Creating a bold ambition, then having the courage, conviction and dogged persistence to achieve it. Legacy leaders understand the hidden potential of defining moments and don't wait for them to happen, but create the the circumstances to bring out greatness in their people and teams. They are tough and exacting, they are paradigm shifters, igniters, revolutionaries and change agents. Ask: What vision is too big to fit in your head, but can only fit in your heart? What is your great unfinished work? What revolution, transformation, or cause can you ignite?

Connection: Having the vulnerability to be known and to know others. Listening and caring deeply; acting and behaving authentically; bringing a sense of humanness to the rational, sometimes coldness of work. Coaching the best in others by deeply listening. Self-sacrificing. They have strong values and character. Ask: Does your team know the real you, your story, in your voice? Do you care deeply about others not for what they can do for you, but because of who they are as people?

Culture: Creating a culture that stands for something meaningful, not a culture of failing but one of growing. Creating a culture of challenge and continuous learning. An environment where people can be themselves and push each other not out of ego, nor personal advancement, but to be better. Creating a culture of positivity and hope, a culture that embraces the imperfection in all of us, and through well accepted standards of excellence, mutual accountability, trust, and deep reliance on each other, a culture that exceeds and wins. Ask: Are you creating the right conditions that brings out the best in them, grows them, and challenges them?

<u>S</u>tories: The way we imprint legacy into our organizations is through stories, actually certain kinds of stories, which we will discover. Stories capture the attention and imagination of audiences; sticky stories cause us to believe, understand and act. Stories have longevity in organizations long after people leave. Stories are carried by people across generations, building a succession of legacy leaders. Ask: What stories do your team members need to hear from you? What are your signature stories?

Triangles are the strongest shape. Not squares, not rectangles. Triangles. Force that comes against triangles is evenly spread among all three sides. Triangles won't collapse easily under pressure. If you want to make squares or cubes stronger, add a diagonal piece across the middle and make it two triangles. The ABC'S of Legacy Building are strongest when each element is proportionately strong compared to the others. Not perfectly proportional —we all have core strengths — but to maximize your legacy potential, you need to leverage your strengths and have a keen eye to work on your shortcomings. The dimensions of legacy are interdependent. Exceptional apprenticing requires an invigorating team culture. Exceptional boldness requires a deep connection of trust and mutual accountability. Stories are the stones of legacy building. The triangle is built moment by moment, story by story.

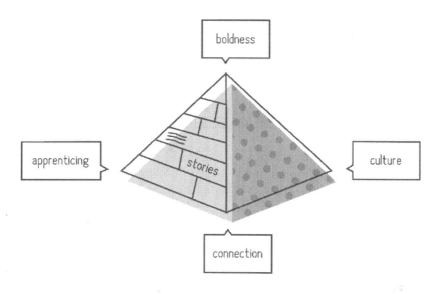

APPRENTICING

Are you a master builder of talent?

The system of apprenticeship was first developed in the Middle Ages through guilds across a wide array of crafts and trades from baking and tailoring to masonry and stonecutting. A master craftsman employed novices as an inexpensive form of labor in exchange for providing food, lodging, and formal training in the craft. Most apprentices aspired to become master craftsmen themselves.

Apprentices usually began at ten to fifteen years of age and would live in the master craftsman's household. He or she would learn not only the hard skills of the trade, but also stalwart values that underpin the person behind the profession. Under the watch of master craftsmen, boys became men and girls became women. The relationship between master craftsman and apprentice was often as close as that between parent and child. An apprentice lived in his master's house or shop; he usually ate with the master's family, often wore clothes provided by the master, and was subject to the master's house rules and discipline. Life-long relationships were formed.

Legacy leaders have more than followers, they have apprentices.

Apprenticing is distinct from leading and managing. Apprenticing involves training and preparing someone for a particular role or profession. The intention is to pass on your knowledge, experiences, and wisdom so they can be competent and skilled to thrive in their profession. Master craftsman didn't just encourage apprentices to try their best; they pursued excellence. They were hard without being harsh; they were exacting without expecting immediate perfection; they were hands-on teachers without sheltering. Generations of trades relied on apprenticing to develop the next generation of master craftsman.

At its core, legacy apprenticing is about imprinting your life skills, know-how, and values so that naiveté is replaced with wisdom. Immaturity withers and responsibility ripens. Apprenticing means you don't protect your apprentices from or hide them from or do for them. You don't pass your problem beginners to someone else; you persistently, unceasingly shape them. Apprenticing prepares your junior team members to be the next generation of master craftsman, the next generation of leaders. But it is something they must earn, something they must achieve, something they will necessarily struggle with.

When master carpenters apprenticed, they were methodical and intentional about the skills of carpentry — flush edges, exacting corner cuts, strong joints. Master builders didn't just ensure their mentees followed their instruction, but they simultaneously explained "why." *"Why do we need to..." Why does it work that way..." Why can't we just..."* Master builders anticipated that their imaginative learners wouldn't blindly follow their rules; that they would seek to satisfy their natural curiosity to be original. The masters taught the principles of their craft and simultaneously stirred the creativity of their apprentices. One master craftsman and his team of apprentices invented vaulted ceilings that became the grandeur in cathedrals. Another master craftsman and his team of apprentices noticed melting sand with metals created colored glass, then designed the first stained glass.

In our hyper-scheduled, busy lives we often feel toxically depleted. We may feel too empty to give anything to anyone. We sometimes prioritize achieving the tangible things — projects and checklists, appointments and deliverables — over the intangibles of teaching, developing, and growing others. But legacy leaders create the margin in their demanding lives to purposefully apprentice others. They pay-it-forward; they give back because someone gave to them. Paradoxically, the antidote for the bitter busyness in our lives isn't getting more done, its focusing on what's most essential and removing everything else as clutter, confusion, and distraction. Management may be one of the most honorable and noble professions when you take the time to grow others, help them realize their fullest potential, release their passions and utilize their unique gifts. People at the top have a disproportionate level of influence over those they lead. Those under them look for cues on what's acceptable, on team norms, and on behaviors to emulate. Apprenticing is the mark of a great leader.

The leaders who people remember, the leaders who made a profound impact on them as a person, the leaders who changed the trajectory of their careers, sometimes their lives; those leaders had something in common. Legacy leaders are great teachers. They consider teaching to be one of their primary roles, they have a teachable point of view and they are incredibly aware of the example they are always projecting. Legacy leaders use every opportunity to grow apprentices into bigger roles, bigger versions of themselves — deeper values, stronger character, unflinching commitment, upskilled capability, remarkable grittiness. One worker said, "They have a true interest and selflessness in helping others grow. Willingness to take the time to mentor others and help them achieve their goals, personal or professional." Another person said, "They truly care and listen. They invested in me when it wasn't' convenient for them." They apprentice one by one by one.

While all of us spend time with co-workers in performance reviews, check-in meetings, and one-on-one meetings, how intentional are we? In *Multipliers*, Liz Wiseman asks: are you enhancing or diminishing their potential? Diminishers underutilize their time with people, leaving them with plenty of action items and busyness, but shallow in passion and hollow in experience. Enhancers ensure they unlock talent by connecting to individual passion. In the rightful spirit of challenging to achieve, Diminishers can be careless with their words, and those words stab like a sword, causing even the most confident co-worker to retreat in self-doubt. But Enhancers expertly challenge others not through finger-pointing or criticizing but by showing their team members how to see with fresh perspectives, sometimes with a wide-angle lens and other times with a telephoto lens. Diminishers tend to be pessimists who react to negative events by explaining them as permanent, personal, and pervasive. Enhancers are optimists who look for limited short-term explanations for bad events, so their team is likely to pick themselves up and try again.

Are you diminishing or enhancing your team? Don't answer too quickly. Listen to the experiences of employees whose leaders were not interested in apprenticing them.

I don't really remember anything much of that year, but I remember everything about what he said one day. Sitting in that conference room when he launched a series of words and phrases that embarrassed me, hurt me, belittled me in front of others. To this day, it still hurts me, still stings.

I lost my self-confidence for years because my leader was either having a bad day, a bad life, or somewhere along the way no one taught him how to engage people not by impatiently criticizing them without listening or offer a better solution...

I remember one week I was working late trying to get a project done for an important client. It seemed like I hadn't seen my family in forever. I received a phone call from my daughter asking if I'd come home to help her with homework. I told my boss that I'd finish up by eight a.m.

tomorrow, but I needed to get home. He really didn't say anything, he didn't need to. He sat at his desk, expressionless, speechless for a really long time...he made me feel terrible.

I hated going to those meetings. No matter how hard we tried to anticipate his questions, he always tossed out a zinger—something no one could answer, something that made us feel stupid, something that in the end didn't matter so much to the project, but mattered to his ego. Somehow, we walked away feeling deflated despite spending weeks developing what we considered a killer plan.

I just never felt like he had our backs. He never fought for us or defended us. He played politics really well, and he soared for a while until they figured him out.

For years I worked for her, but in a strange way, she never got to know me. I don't even mean on the personal side...not what I am passionate about, not the kind of work I love to do, not what I want next in my career and my life. Our meetings were abrupt, if things were going well, then she seemed passively satisfied, and if things were off a bit then she'd push to get it done. Nothing much more or less than that. It was as if I was a machine not a person.

Now contrast those quotes with stories about leaders who took their team apprenticing to heart.

I remember sitting in the meeting room surprised that my boss deflected all of the credit to me. Gushed over my tireless work and deep thinking, going over all the details, I didn't even know he knew what I was working on. He THANKED me with such sincerely and specificity. I remember walking back to my desk with a little bit of swagger. I've carried that encouragement into almost every assignment after that.

To say I was reluctant to take the bigger role is an understatement. But she took a chance on me and wanted me to stretch myself. So I jumped into the unknown. She didn't leave me hanging. She coached me constantly—sometimes giving me the encouragement I needed and other times challenging me to think differently. She worked alongside me, teaching me enough of the fundamentals to do the work I wasn't clearly skilled for. I learned more about myself that year than ever in my career.

It was a monumental set-back. The entire project team was crushed. How would we recover from this? I still remember him pulling us together early one morning with a cup of coffee, a smile and fierce determination. He told us a story about one of his first moments of doubt and despair at work and how it was a turning point for him. I tend to be negative and doubtful when it comes to these types of things, but his positivity and resolve was infectious. For weeks we poured our lives into fixing what seemed permanently broken. I've carried that same positive attitude and determination into some tough assignments since then.

Are you a master craftsman who diminishes or enhances your team? Tell a story about a time when you were a Diminisher or worked for someone who diminished you. Tell a story about a time when you were an Enhancer or worked for someone who enhanced you.

Tell a story about when you made the change from Diminisher to Enhancer — what was the lightbulb moment and what did you start and stop doing?

The Keys to Effective Apprenticing

There are signature apprenticing characteristics of master craftsman. How you purposefully apprentice, not just lead effectively nor just manage well, but invest in people, shapes and develops them to be better.

Stretches others and brings out the best in people. Why can some employees have a can-do attitude, act proactively and with accountability under one leader but then be cautious, defensive, and almost incompetent under another leader? Some leaders expand abilities. They provide us with opportunities that give us that sinking feeling called personal growth. They unlock our giftedness. Some leaders make us smarter and better; they bring out the best in us, our greatness—our natural abilities, our natural instincts, our natural intelligence, our natural passions. They bolster our natural extrinsic strengths—what we accomplish from talent and hard work. And they also help us connect to our intrinsic strengths—what gives us energy. Legacy leaders elicit discretionary, voluntary ingenuity and effort, the kind that cannot be bought or forced, only invited and encouraged. One worker said, "You can tell they care about you not only as a member of the team, but as a person and you find yourself working harder and trying to emulate them."

Master craftsman believe that intelligence isn't fixed but can change over time; they encourage a growth mindset versus fixed mindset, ensuring their apprentices expand their capabilities, continually developing their abilities. One of the most fundamental elements of being a leader is stretching others to achieve seemingly impossible tasks, new capabilities, broad discoveries.

We all have unique gifts, personality traits that seem to enhance others, matchless skills that set us apart, and passionate interests that enliven our hearts. But many of those unique gifts are undiscovered, underutilized, and unappreciated because these talents are buried underneath the rubble of collapsed self-impressions or submarined deep inside us because they don't align with culturally accepted stereotypes of success. Countless people unintentionally suppress their greatness and passion. Some aren't aware of their gifts. Some of those gifts are never even opened. Your apprenticing can illuminate the greatness you see in your team members and co-workers. You can encourage them to take a peek at their unopened gifts. Are you the kind of leader who sees the greatness in others and has thought deeply about how to release it?

Something is stretched when it is caught between two opposing positions: stasis and breaking. Sometimes being afraid of breaking causes us to stay still or hold back. Stretching grows us and extends us to a point where it hurts a little. Some people need a nudge to stretch.

I was in Operations. Pretty good at it too. Had a few promotions. Almost the only female manager across our manufacturing plants, certainly one of the most senior. One day my boss asked me to take an assignment in marketing. Marketing...oh no! I never saw myself as creative; I was an introvert and I hated the inexactness of marketing. I prided myself in numbers, felt safe around numbers, targets, clear challenges not the existentialism of marketing. And I was doing well in operations – I was making a name for myself. I resisted for quite some time, and then he asked me to trust him and I was just reassigned. I'm so glad my boss saw something in me that I didn't see, because it changed my professional life and unleashed a passion in me that has allowed me to go to work excited every day for ten years...

Are tough and exacting. Master craftsman set high expectations for themselves and everyone around them. They ask questions not to show who's smarter, but to pressure-test rigor. They challenge their team not to find fault, but to advance the thinking. They finely balance pouring over the details with care without micro-managing people.

Following the disaster of Apollo flight 1, when astronauts Gus Grissom, Ed White and Roger Chaffee were killed in a fire during a training exercise, Gene Kranz, NASA Flight Director, called a meeting of his branch and flight control team. He addressed them with a speech that has imprinted "NASA, tough and competent" onto legions of scientists and engineers who have worked there since. It has been called the Kranz Dictum.

Spaceflight will never tolerate carelessness, incapacity, and neglect. Somewhere, somehow, we screwed up. It could have been in design, build, or test. Whatever it was, we should have caught it. We were too gung ho about the schedule, and we locked out all of the problems we saw each day in our work. Every element of the program was in trouble and so were we. The simulators were not working, Mission Control was behind in virtually every area, and the flight and test procedures changed daily. Nothing we did had any shelf life. Not one of us stood up and said, "Dammit, stop!" I don't know what Thompson's committee will find as the cause, but I know what I find. We are the cause! We were not ready! We did not do our job. We were rolling the dice, hoping that things would come together by launch day, when in our hearts we knew it would take a miracle. We were pushing the schedule and betting that the Cape would slip before we did.

From this day forward, Flight Control will be known by two words: "Tough" and "Competent." Tough means we are forever accountable for what we do or what we fail to do. We will never again compromise our responsibilities. Every time we walk into Mission Control we will know what we stand for. Competent means we will never take anything for granted. We will never be found short in our knowledge and in our skills. Mission Control will be perfect. When you leave this meeting today you will go to your office and the first thing you will do there is to write "Tough and Competent" on your blackboards. It will never be erased. Each day when you enter the room these words will remind you of the price paid by Grissom, White, and Chaffee. These words are the price of admission to the ranks of Mission Control.

Legacy leaders have an expectation of excellence. They do hard things, things at the edge of the team's ability, but they deliberately practice, make mistakes, to become better. They rarely quit and when they do, it's only at natural stopping points when practical options have been exhausted. They hold the output of their work in high esteem, not in a prideful way, but in a deeply personal way. After all, the mark of a master craftsman is his or her work.

Are you a leader who raises the bar on performance, known to be tough and exacting when the stakes are high?

Grows a tree of talent. Legacy leaders spawn other leaders. One worker said, "They have a consistent desire to mentor and coach the next generation of leaders." In the 2015-16 NFL season, out of thirty-two teams, twenty had a coach who came from the Bill Walsh tree of talent. Bill Walsh finished coaching the NFL in 1989 and died in 2007. In highly successful organizations, there is a chain of great performers, bold thinkers, astute apprentices who emerged as pivotal figures from master builders. Sydney Finkelstein at Wharton calls them "superbosses." These superbosses are "always teaching — they prowl around looking for people to take on more responsibility." Legacy leaders are talent magnets. They attract talented people because their reputation pulls people into their orbit. In a free agency mindset, great leaders attract followers who want to become great leaders. Legacy leaders are always in the quarry mining for talent gems through stretch assignments, coffee chats, and mentoring.

Legacy leaders place confidence in others by delegating responsibility, tough decisions, tense negotiations usually before apprentices feel they are ready. They take a chance on people not by walking away to see how they measure up, but by walking behind them or alongside them to watch them rise or to pick them up when they stumble.

Betting on someone is rarely a guaranteed fortuitous outcome. When you trust people to step into bigger leadership roles, they are never perfectly prepared, never fully ready, never without risk of failure.

Sharing Center Stage

"I want you to present the project," he said. I was dumbfounded. It was one of the most successful endeavors in years and my manger wanted me to take the spotlight...at a time when he needed it most. He had been sorely criticized for some decisions he had made; he sheltered us from a tremendous amount of pressure. I know he desperately wanted the redemption – to prove them wrong, to prove his leadership. But today, this day when the praise would be directed to the team presenter, he wanted me to have it. Later that year, when our team won "Impact-of-the-Year" award across the entire company, I saw his face beaming in the crowd, taking pictures like a proud parent and I could see that was satisfaction enough for him. A few years later when I became a team leader, I knew exactly how I wanted to show up.

Are you a tree of talent? When you look around your organization, do you see your leadership DNA? Are you preparing your team to be the next generation of leaders?

Instills ownership and nobly shares the best inside them. Master builders share their talent and intellect, ideas and energy. They give others enough training and the right tools to get the job done as well as take ownership of the results. They have a personal stake in ensuring apprentices have enough space to grow and learn. The result: ideas blossom, challenges are tackled, hard problems are solved, accountability is shared. Andy Grove, former CEO of Intel, recalls a time when he nearly made a tragic decision, but one of his apprentices courageously warned him of the consequences. "We almost wrecked the company. We had established our technology as the industry standard. But I almost walked away from it because the elegance of the new product seduced me into taking my eye off the market," said Grove. (Fortune, Intel: The education of Andy Grove. 3/21/2016)

Legacy leaders sacrifice. They choose to work alongside us, with us, for us. They see leadership as a privilege that requires placing the duties of others above their own self-interest. They prioritize the needs of their team and in return their team gives their best. They have a servant mindset — offering help, providing advice, putting others in the spotlight. They are self-less; there is less of them and more of others. One worker said, "[Legacy] leaders put the business and their teams before themselves...focused on the good of the company and others even at the selfless expense of themselves."

Everyone needs an inspiration, somebody who can really help them see what's possible, a role model to look up to. Apprentices savor exposure to the master craftsman — hands-on time, guiding their chisels, hammering iron, blowing glass. Legacy leaders selflessly dedicate time, care and effort to others; they find deep joy by sharing their talents and meeting the needs of others because of a genuine willingness to put service for others and the organization before their own self-interests. They take the heat for their team often putting themselves in the crosshairs of ridicule when the results aren't immediate or auspicious. One worker observed, "[she] invested first-thing Friday mornings in me because she had a genuine interest in seeing me succeed."

> I was struggling. She could see that. Everyone could see that. Instead of replacing me with someone who could clearly handle the project better, she meet with me over coffee once a week for months. She was committed to me not failing. She never did the work for me or swooped in to solve my problems, but she coached me on how to think through motivating the team and removing the barriers holding us back. She refused to let me quit. She believed in me and sincerely wanted to see me succeed even though it was inconvenient for her. I gave her everything I could...to turn this project around.

Are you telling or teaching, co-creating or critiquing, blossoming or browbeating? Are you a leader who makes everyone around you smarter, shrewder, more capable? Do your actions show that others come first? Does it show up that way in your schedule?

Takes a chance on people. Master builders see something in apprentices that the apprentices can't see in themselves. The master builder believes in them when they don't believe in themselves. Legacy leaders look for the underdogs; they seek out the overlooked in the land of misfit toys. They can see potential over pedigree, raw talent that needs chiseling, roughened around the edges that needs smoothing. They are devoted to eager apprentices who are teachable. They give their apprentices space to try out new things, they consider mistakes as explorations in learning, not blame for inadequacy.

Tom Watson Jr., CEO of IBM between 1956 and 1971, was a key figure in the information revolution. Watson repeatedly demonstrated his abilities as a legacy leader forging the new era of information technology, but he was also a savvy people-developer. One example is the story of a young executive who had made some bad decisions that cost the company several million dollars. He was summoned to Watson's office, fully expecting to be dismissed. As he entered the office, the young executive said, "I suppose after that set of mistakes you will want to fire me." Watson was said to have replied, "Not at all, young man. We have just spent a couple of million dollars educating you." (Schein, 2016)

Who, when they look back, will say that you took a chance on them?

Has a teachable point of view. Master craftsman can clearly articulate their ideas, values and experience into lessons. It's not enough to have knowledge; apprentices need to draw lessons from your experiences through your unique set of leadership principles — your leadership code. The ability to do something well and the ability to articulate how to do it are two different skills, so master builders take time to organize their thoughts to communicate clearly. They constantly think about their experiences and draw lessons from them, storing them in the form of stories that they use to guide their own decisions but also teach others.

Do you have a teachable point of view from which you draw lessons and stories?

Has stalwart character traits. Character traits that matter so much to success are not entirely innate. They don't appear in us magically as a result of good luck or good genes. They can be modeled and shaped in us by the context of our work environment. Paul Tough, author of *How Children Succeed*, says, "What matters most in a child's development...is not how much information we can stuff into her brain in the first few years. What matters, instead, is whether we are able to help her develop a very different set of qualities, a list that includes persistence, self-control, curiosity, conscientiousness, grit, and self-confidence." Development of these traits, and others like resilience and collaboration, integrity and trustworthiness, don't magically cease to be important when you enter the doors of your first job. Social scientists have found that you get many of these character traits through failure, through defeat, through the act of trying hard things, and especially through the social culture of organizations.

The character of the organization is established by the character of the people who work there and that character is determined by the leader. Legacy leaders are driven by fundamental, undeniable principles deeply engrained in them. Their heights of intellect are matched by the depths of their character. One worker said, "[positive legacy leaders] have a dedication to results without deforming their character." How they conduct work, how they show up, how they produce is just as important as what they produce.

Legacy leaders lead from the inside out. Character is more important than persona. Their actions originate from deep within themselves not superficially in protecting their personality and image. A leader's character is determined by his motives and his motives are always a matter of the heart, because it's in our heart where our deepest values and convictions are held. We don't really develop our core convictions as much as they develop within us through experiences and the social culture around us. Legacy leaders set the team or organizational culture that reinforces character traits and allows them to flourish.

"You're looking for three things, generally, in a person," says Warren Buffett. "Intelligence, energy, and integrity. And if they don't have the last one, don't even bother with the first two. Integrity is up to you. You weren't born with it, you can't learn it in school. You decide to be dishonest, stingy, uncharitable, egotistical, all the things people don't like in other people. They are all choices. Some people think there's a limited little pot of admiration to go around, and anything the other guy takes out of the pot, there's less left for you."

Do you model the character traits you hold tight? Does your example amplify it in others?

Fosters Grittiness. In her late twenties, Angela Duckworth left a demanding job as a management consultant to teach math to seventh graders in the New York City public schools. Several years in the classroom taught her that effort was tremendously important to success. To begin to solve the mystery of why some people work so much harder and longer than others, Angela entered the Ph.D. program in psychology at the University of Pennsylvania, where she is now a professor. She wrote the best-selling book, *Grit: The Power of Passion and Perseverance*.

By studying the gamut of achievers — from spelling bee winners to West Point cadets, whiz kids from Silicon Valley to impoverished achievers in inner cities — Duckworth identified the traits of gritty people: *passion* — sustained enduring devotion to distant goals in the future — and *perseverance* — persistence amid rejection. Legacy leaders help apprentices find their passion by developing and deepening interest in a wide array of pursuits over time; they expose them to special projects and put them in new circumstances to help them discover their passion through trial and error. Legacy leaders don't let their apprentices abandon tasks in the face of obstacles; they nurture strength of will and build perseverance. They don't cultivate perfectionism, but they provide hope — believing in something you can do to positively change your future.

Do you help others discover their passion? Do you ensure they don't give up too early and lean into doing hard things at the edge of their ability?

Guards others' hearts. Negative legacy leaders love to criticize. They seem to find fault with the work of others and thrive on correcting their mistakes. They love pointing out errors. One worker said, "[they] sit in judgement with a red pen in hand. They are quick to judge and slow to compliment and encourage." Instead of working to get the best answers, collaborating on deep strategic questions and partnering on finding insights in a sea of data, some leaders simply put their effort in finding errors; they are intellectual bullies.

Master craftsman know the hearts of those they apprentice. While walking beside them, behind them, in front of them, they have an ever-watchful eye for what's happening inside them. They know that the way to unlock an apprentice's potential is through their heart, not their head, that the condition of their heart is a key determinant of their future. Legacy leaders are quick to catch envy, reckless ambition, self-defeat or negativity before it damages apprentice's heart while also ensuring healthy doses of encouragement, positivity and acceptance.

Master builders notice; they pay attention to the person and the job. Noticing allows you to appreciate the details that can easily get lost in a hurried day. Noticing allows you, with the precision of a master craftsman, to recognize not just the achievement, but the effort. It's a lifelong need — to be noticed by our mentors. Few things are more gratifying for apprentices then to be appreciated by their master builders.

Do you notice your team members beyond the achievement, before the result? Do you watch the condition of others' hearts, not just the skill in their head or hands?

Label and Re-Label Apprentices. Words can build others up or tear them down. A sarcastic comment can shred your apprentice's confidence. An encouraging statement can invigorate them. Your words matter. They aren't neutral. Words carry emotion and meaning behind them whether you are intentional about them or not. Few words are more personally impactful than those from leaders. Words from leaders are powerful; they can change the trajectory of personal and professional lives; they can spur turning points.

Words unsaid matter too. Your absence of words — missed opportunities for words of gratitude and appreciation, affirmation and encouragement — can sting as much as hurtful words said. Silence signals ambivalence and apathy. Are you stingy with your praise?

We live in a world defined by labels. Brands symbolize and say something when we wear them, drive them, use them. We are label-conscious. We carry around labels too, and they can define our identity. Someone else's opinion can mark you. If you look closely enough, you can see the labels affixed to people. You can see the badges they wear — "ugly," "arrogant snob," "stupid," "undependable," "lazy," "chicken," "selfish," "angry," "callous," "courageous," "thoughtful," "considerate," "kind," "generous," "clever," "cheerful," "mentor," "helpful," "gentle," "team builder," "maximizer of talent," "loyal," "optimist."

If we are honest with ourselves, we all carry around labels. Someone's words have defined us. Some words of affirmation have been badges of honor that we have lived up to, while some harsh, unfair words have crushed our spirits. The words from master builders to apprentices carry weight. We live up to or live down to the labels others have placed on us especially when they were placed there by our leaders and peers. These words can become self-fulfilling.

Overtly notice behaviors you want repeated again. Label them positively. Affix them to people and teams so they wear their labels proudly. They will wear the label again and they will want to live up to the label. Let them know that you see the good labels fitting nicely on them like a beautiful dress or a clean, crisp shirt. Let them know that they look stunning in it.

Help them to remove any negative labels. We all carry the ego bruises under the deadfall of careless, callous words that became twisted self-beliefs. Reframe their self-limiting beliefs. Re-label them and forge positive identities that unlock their potential, so they can see themselves differently. Master craftsmen create authentic, positive self-perceptions that can overcome apprentices' distorted self-images, insecurities and stigmas. Help your apprentices to see the everyday events in their work lives not just as random circumstances, but as extraordinary opportunities to make a difference in the lives of customers and co-workers. Let them see you cheering them on. Let them know that you believe in them. Let them know that your company, your team, you rely on them.

How would you introduce your team to a new customer, to the new leader? We live up to the honor of our introductions. What if how you introduced them actually became what they strived for; what they lived up to? What if you revealed what longings you had for them, what you hoped for in them, what qualities you admired in them, what gratitude you had for them? Prompt them to live lives worthy of labels they proudly want to carry.

Starting my work life as a junior accountant, was a very different career path than I had originally envisaged for myself. I was a young female in a large corporate environment with the energy to learn and grow and progress on to bigger and better things, but at the same time vulnerable, impressionable and to a certain extent a little naïve.

After a short time I was asking my line manager how I could get to the next level in the organization. Her response to my question was, "Quite honestly, I think you have a vision way above your station. You were bought in here to work as a junior accountant, and that is where you are likely to end up." There it was, put right out there; she saw no potential in me. Someone I was supposed to be managed, coached, influenced, and encouraged by had delivered such a negative and unsupported claim. That statement had such a detrimental effect on me and stayed with me for years. Honestly, it destroyed the little self-confidence I had. Her voice stayed inside my head for years and was like having someone constantly telling me that I wasn't good enough.

My confidence was so low that I was physically unable to speak in a room of people; even just a few would fill me with dread. But then I had a new manager who encouraged me, "You have potential and you have heart, you deliver, you have a can-do attitude, you have a natural curiosity and a way of simplifying complexity. Now, let's work on your self-confidence." Someone was willing to take a chance on me.

That line manager pushed me out of just about every comfort zone I had, but with a sense of nurture, support and encouragement that gave me strength, self-belief, and enough confidence to try new things. I started to achieve more demanding roles. On one occasion he asked me to present on a topic at our annual global leadership conference for about fifty of my peers and a dozen senior leaders of the business. Old tapes starting coming back — what if I am not good enough and I don't meet their expectations?

That day I presented from the heart with passion, conviction and from the real me. When I finished, the round of applause, was immense. My manager and mentor came up to me after the session was complete and said, "I am so proud of what you have just achieved." Now, those words stay with me.

Legacy Story Starters

What labels are affixed to you? Tell a story about how a master craftsman affixed a positive label on you that made a tremendous difference in your life.

What labels are affixed to those on your team or apprentices? What do you want them to see in themselves? What labels do you want removed and replaced? Place a new label on them and write a new core narrative for them by telling a story of them at their best.

Apprenticing is a verb

Apprenticing requires work, sacrifice, resolve. There are dozens of other things we could do with our time besides spending it in selfless service to others. Apprenticing is servant leadership. Todd Carmichael, co-founder of La Colombe, one of the most successful artisan coffee roasters in America, asks his favorite question in job interviews: "Give me an example of how you've improved the career of someone else?" We must listen carefully to our apprentices' problems when we have our own. We must help apprentices who are stuck when our own work is piled up. In the busyness of life, who will you inconveniently teach? What impression will you make on them so they thank you...not from a stage or with a round of applause but in quiet conversation with heartfelt gratitude?

There are few things more fulfilling then watching apprentices take a bow and come up taller. Despite having started from practically nothing, despite being passed over, shoved aside, having had a disadvantaged start, under the watchful eye, the steady hand and careful words of legacy leaders, even the most unlikely of people can sprout, blossom, develop.

I started from nothing. No skills, no degree. My three brothers and I were raised by a single mom in "the projects." So when he hired me, I was more than appreciative; he saved me. I worked hard — no one out-worked me — cleaning floors, perfecting the store shelves, ensuring the trash never reached the top of the bin, attending to every detail. He started showing me new things. The cash register, the stockroom, things on the computer — spreadsheets, numbers. I soaked it up like a sponge.

I noticed something about him — he always smiled. Smiled at customers. Smiled at me. Smiled when lifting boxes and taking out the trash. I never used to smile. Really, I had nothing to smile about. But his smile was contagious. And I found myself smiling back at him, back at customers, back at life. He always gave me a little more than I could handle. Sometimes I'd mess up, but never in the same way twice, because he'd teach me to do better next time. He'd shake his head once in a while, but he never lost his cool and he never stopped giving me more responsibility.

Then one day he gave me the keys — the keys to open in the morning and close at night. Man, I tell you, nothing felt so...(tearing)...nothing gave me more pride. After a while, I was running the place. Customers knew me. Truck drivers knew me. New employees asked me for advice and to show them how to get things done. And I showed them just like he showed me. Now I know what he was smiling about. If you want to know why I smile, why I'm so cheerful, it's because I used to be that bitter boy and I'm not anymore.

Legacy Story Starters

Who made a dent in your life? Who are you incredibly grateful to? People want to see not just your journey, but who helped you along the way. Are you humble enough to recognize them and are you prepared to pay it forward? Who mentored you; was a role model for you; made a deep impression on your life? What invaluable lessons did they teach you?

Are you improving the career of someone else – not just someone reporting to you?

BOLDNESS

What dream is too big to fit inside your head, but can only fit in your immense heart?

I can tell you with certainty, it's not nailing the big deal, delivering your stretch sales goal, having more 'likes' for your social media campaign or delivering the project three weeks early. Those are important in the present but never lasting enough for legacy building. Boldness is sparked with a vision, a passion, a conviction that pulls you and others toward a dimly lit, yet hopeful future.

Legacy leaders have personal humility coupled with an indomitable will toward a cause that's bigger than themselves. Jim Collins in *Good to Great* calls this Level 5 Leadership. They self-impose a level of inadequacy that pulls their apprentices, their team, their entire organization toward a bold, out-in-front ambition that can only be achieved when all of us must learn, must change, must grow. Organizations infected with the disease of mediocrity need an ambition to greatness. Legacy leaders understand the art of getting people to do what needs to be done. One worker said, "[Positive legacy leaders] have the ability to outpace everyone else without stepping on people and/or making others feel insignificant about their own contributions at work. They know the vision and mission of the company, they craft a strategy and they empower their directs to put together an execution plan that delivers."

Forged at the intersection of a hopeful vision, a deep desire for meaningful change, and steadfast character traits, legacy leaders imprint boldness. It's often testing and trying circumstances that illuminate the hidden character traits and bring out the legacy leader in us. You'd never pick some of the most impressive legacy leaders to charge a rebellion. Many are far too gentle, but they feel called to live the words they believe. These are the torchbearers we follow even if the road is dimly lit. As one worker said in one of my interviews, "Most people can help the business achieve or exceed their goals. To me leaving legacy is all about the way you do it...clarity of vision and the bold perseverance to carry it out."

The Torchbearer's Boldness Characteristics

A leader's role is to define reality and then give hope. Legacy leaders are torchbearers lighting the way for people to reach an uncommon goal. They demonstrate to others that their work is more than checking the boxes. Their quest is heroic. Legacy torchbearers aren't out to prove their heroism, but to claim it. The idea of proving heroism is tied up in the false notion that courage is a scarce commodity and that there is a hierarchy of people who are entitled to it. The circumstances create the opportunity for leaders to emerge, and those aren't pre-destined for just some of us. But a legacy story is written when a leader makes a choice to lean in or hold back, to face into or turn away from challenges. Boldness is available for all of us; here are some characteristics of boldness exemplified by legacy leaders:

Catalyst for Disruptive Change. Legacy leaders turn fear into faith. In many cases, they lean into organizations and teams that are in distress. When the going gets tough, some people flee rather than roll-up-their sleeves and work on improving the organization. When the stakes are high, there is often a silent retreat. Apathy has caused scores of people to choose personal survival over collective responsibility.

Negative legacy leaders sometimes make decisions to protect egos and avoid the loss of status. On the other hand, positive legacy leaders generate hope when others appear worn out, frustrated with politics, and callous toward "another" change. They push our thinking. As one worker said, "They champion disruptive thinking that leads to transformational change."

Amid tense circumstances, legacy torchbearers act outside the expected scripts and operating constraints of their industry. They begin with the assumption that change is possible. They are willing to speak up about a wrong or injustice, about what could be better before knowing how to make things better. Todd

Carmichael of La Colombe Coffee Roasters said, "I've spent a lot of time searching for coffee in places that people warn against, like war zones and areas recovering from natural disaster. Places where we can make a difference." With no certainty, no quick answers, no guarantees, legacy leaders replace cynicism with positivity. They replace resignation with resolute action. They don't wait for issues to become someone else's responsibility; rather, they inspire a small band of revolutionaries to make it their responsibility. When they see a problem, they own it.

Most companies don't match their bold aspirations with bold actions. Common are the companies with big ambitions, but few are the companies that drive them with persistence, rigor, determination into real plans with real consequences and real results. A McKinsey study found that to make a major leap in performance, companies need to make big, bold moves across multiple fronts (Chris Bradley, 2018). Incremental moves don't get companies very far. In fact, incrementalism may actually increase the risk of stagnation.

Wendell Weeks Makes Bold Moves at Corning

Corning was a paragon of innovation - from developing the glass in Thomas Edison's lightbulb to producing fiber-optic cables that dawned the digital age. But when Wendell Weeks took over as CEO in 2005, Corning was a mess. The dot-com bubble burst, telecommunications had been hit quite hard and Corning was no exception. Revenues were cut in half, soaring profits became losses, and Corning's share price plummeted 99% in 2002 from its peak in September of 2000.

Under Weeks's leadership Corning made a bold move into a market-leading position in LCD displays years before they had become mainstream in televisions. Corning also made a bold move in mobile device glass. While Corning had invented and invested heavily into Gorilla Glass despite severe financial austerity, the market for smartphones and mobile devices was minute. But Weeks invested massively ahead of the market. Now Gorilla Glass is designed into more than 4.5 billion smartphones, tablets, and other handheld electronic devices.

Where do you need to be on the forefront of change? How can you spark a revolution in your company, your category?

Ask Propelling Questions. Legacy torchbearers don't simply check the boxes in an effort to get things done. They deliver impact. Much of the time, the impact is unexpected because the approach was unconventional.

In our ambition to fix brokenness we move rapidly with the same outmoded plays in the playbook. In the face of disruption or stagnation, the seeds of destruction may be built into the very DNA of our success. The strategies, the processes, the culture, the schemas that collectively led to a company's success amassed over years or decades can easily become an inflexible devotion to how things get done and what must remain even in the face of an urgent need to change. Legacy torchbearers tackle intractable, self-limiting beliefs with a poised revolutionary charge. They exercise small acts of rebellious disobedience to the status quo. They break paradigms by framing questions in way that propels thinking off the traditional path.

Legacy leaders ask us to be unreasonable by asking propelling questions. In *A Beautiful Constraint*, authors Adam Morgan and Mark Barden introduce the concept of Propelling Questions. Propelling Questions intersect a bold ambition with a significant constraint so requests seem unreasonable, nearly impossible, but their unreasonableness pushes against the edges — the edges of discovery, the edges of the familiar — so that habitual ways of solving problems are abandoned. Legacy leaders embrace the power of the edge by asking propelling questions that reframe our thinking beyond what is reasonable. When Audi entered the Le Mans 24-hour race in 2006, the traditional question of the racing industry was how can we build a faster car? A faster car inevitably equates to winning. Yet, Audi was competing with teams with bigger budgets, deeper racing capability in Le Mans. Everyone was trying to build the fastest car. So Audi had to ask itself a different question. A propelling question that closely linked their ambition (to win the race) with their constraint (lack of resources to build a faster car). "How could we win Le Mans if our car could go no faster than anyone else's?" This propelling question saw them enter the R10 TDI, a diesel fuel-powered car. The answer to their propelling question was fuel efficiency. Stopping less for fuel despite a slightly slower car allowed Audi to win the Le Mans race for the next three consecutive years (A Beautiful Constraint, 2015).

IKEA is known for this approach. How can you make and produce a well-designed, durable table profitably for 5 euros? Unreasonable – yes. You can't use the same approach as before. You can't look to your left or right at what competitors are doing. You need a multi-disciplinary approach — from supply chain to materials to design and packaging — to birth a new mindset and break paradigms.

Legacy leaders steer the organization toward constraints not away from them, even setting up artificial constraints. They get their teams to master the transition from victim (oh-woe-is-me) to transformer (let's tackle this head-on) by apprenticing them with the right growth mindset, the right push toward the edge, the right ambitious target, the intrepid spirit of pioneers. In the process they get people to believe it is possible.

The Cat in the Hat

When William Spaulding, the head of Houghton Mifflin's education division, invited Theodore Geisel, better known as Dr. Seuss, to dinner, he asked him to "write me a story that first graders can't put down." His request came with a list of words he was to use; intending to ride the wave of phonics as a new way to educate children with the sounds that letters and groups of letters makes so they could figure out unfamiliar words themselves. Spaulding wanted a story written using a vocabulary of just 225 words. The *Cat in the Hat* was an immediate success — it transformed books and the nature of primary reading. When the head of Random House bet Geisel he couldn't write a book with just 50 words, he wrote *Green Eggs and Ham* which uses 49 one-syllable words and the word *anywhere*. It became the best-selling Dr. Seuss book ever (Morgan, 2015).

What routines, mindsets, paradigms need to be re-considered, overthrown, revolted against? What self-limiting beliefs are holding your organization back? What propelling questions should you be asking from your organization or team?

Illuminate A Bold, Meaningful Vision. We were made to dream. Dreams don't lie in your comfort zone; they always feel out of reach. Little dreams can fit in our head, but big dreams can only fit in our hearts. Those are the dreams our teams are looking for from us. Few of us have ever told another person what our dream is. It is just too precious, too fragile, too impossible to believe so we keep it hidden, buried inside us. But that's not where you find legacy.

Legacy torchbearers build according to a plan that started with an intention in their hearts and then became a personal quest. If you say you're about something, then what activities in your work, in your company indicate the conviction behind the words? What vision do you have for your work, your profession, your organization, your community? What vision or dream still makes your heart swell with anticipation and hope and possibility? Even if your vision may be dormant, it's not dead. Dust it off. Grab ahold of it. Pursue it. Don't shrink it down based on how you see your ability. Let it pull you forward into a future you desperately want for your teams, your apprentices, your community, your organization, yourself.

Spencer Nix was an evangelical pastor when he started helping a friend, Nick Downs, brew small batches of beer in his basement. Friends and newcomers joined them on Friday evenings where the gatherings grew to more than 100 people communing over beer. That's the unlikely beginning of one of the fastest growing micro-beer breweries in the Southeast – Reformation Brewery. The business name refers to the Protestant movement sparked by Martin Luther. The Reformation team sees craft beer as a way for people to join together, not unlike the way people did in the formative years of the Protestant movement (Kempner, 2016). Reformation holds fast to its values like authenticity, humor, moderation, acceptance, humility and story while advocating to *set beer free*. As Nix says, "We believe beer is a very good gift. Like any gift, it's to be savored and enjoyed. Not necessarily because you've earned it, but because it's truly a blessing. We, largely as a people, don't take time to cherish our blessings today. Everything is so busy, rushed, temporary, offensive, low-grade, and forced. We want to elevate the experience around well-made beer, so we are intentionally minimal with our brand as we see it as such a stark contrast to our surroundings. "Set Beer Free" is about liberating the good gift of beer from institutional tastes, intolerable trends, and social extremes." (Semrau, 2015)

We all crave meaning, crave to be part of something big, something bigger than ourselves. Legacy torchbearers make their vision happen by getting it off a piece of paper and often acting in unexpected, unreasonable ways in order to make that vision happen. One worker said, "[Legacy leaders] set a bold vision, and passionately persevere, empowering and inspiring others to bring it to life, breaking down barriers to change, while doing this positively and authentically. They are open and listen to the feedback of others at all levels."

Disrupting Elder Care

Dr. Bill Thomas is an elder-care abolitionist. In 2008, the *Wall Street Journal* named Dr. Bill among the twelve most influential Americans who are shaping aging in the 21st century. Thomas and his wife, Judith, developed the Eden Alternative, a radical approach to de- institutionalize elders living in the sterile, lifeless environments of long-term care facilities. Thomas was an ER physician when he took a part-time job in a nursing home early in his medical profession. "I took the job and immediately sensed some important work I was meant to do," says Dr. Bill. "I began to see loneliness, helplessness and boredom. I began to see the importance these three plagues were having in the lives of elders. I dreamed of changing the lives of elders and rid them of these plagues...this led to Eden Alternative."

Eden Alternative challenged the status quo in long-term care and offered a creative way to "change the culture" of nursing homes by bringing growth, dignity, companionship, and laughter into the lives of elders. Thomas imagined a new approach to long-term care, known as Green Houses. Green Houses are based on fundamental changes to elder care. Instead of a traditional group home reminiscent of a hospital with dozens if not over one hundred residents, a Green House community consists of clusters of smaller homes (often in residential areas) with six to twelve elders in each cluster. Immediately, you notice things that aren't typically seen in nursing homes — pets, gardens, an open kitchen, small children, decorations. Elders have the freedom to bathe when they want, not a once-a-week opportunity in an overcrowded schedule. There's an open kitchen with staff making dinner and elders have the freedom to make a sandwich on their own. You also notice what is lacking — no long stark corridors of cinder blocks, medication carts and a community bathing room.

Most impressive are the outcomes: $1,300 to $2,300 less in total Medicare and Medicaid costs per resident over twelve months in Green Houses vs. traditional nursing homes, 22-31 minutes more direct care time per elder per day with four times more staff engagement, seven percent higher overall occupancy. More importantly 95% of consumers favor Green Houses over traditional nursing homes (White Paper – The Green House Project, 2018).

What are your dreams for your teams and organization, for your community? Where do you need to start being unreasonable?

Courageous Decision to Heed the Call. Legacy leaders make the tough decision to walk from the familiar, the comfortable, the expected, to the unfamiliar, the risky, the unexpected. Often, their against-the-grain decisions are met with resistance. But they act courageously — to heed the call, to leap, to charge forward. Brash arrogance isn't it. Cavalier bravado isn't it. But standing alone with to resolute convictions, making well-considered, strategic decisions: that's what it's about. Legacy torchbearers have an insurgency mission, a persistence of motive. They redefine the rules in their industry or category not in a self-serving way, but in order to benefit underserved customers.

Legacy torchbearers make the tough calls in the face of tense, seemingly impossible, no-win situations, when something significant is on the line. They demand candor and bluntness in search of the unbiased truth. Legacy leaders ask the questions often no one else is courageous enough to ask.

CEO Walked Out the Door of one Company and Came Back to a New One

It's far too easy to forget how hard-won Intel's success has been. Andy Grove led Intel through one of the most critical decisions, which shook the foundations of the stalwart company in the mid-80s. Left in the hands of someone less demanding, strong-willed —"paranoid," as Grove would call it — it might not have happened at all.

Grove coined the phrase *strategic infection point* to describe an order of magnitude change in the company's environment which creates opportunities to either go way up or way down; at these points management must make a decision. Intel's primary business in the mid-80's was memory chips; it was the lifeblood and original business of Intel, but they were losing significant share to less expensive Japanese memory-chip makers.

Andy had to take himself and his own baggage out of the picture. Many people were too invested in memory chips to see that it had become a commodity and mounting losses were draining the company. "During that time, we worked hard without a clear notion of how things were going to get better. We had lost our bearings. We were wandering in the valley of death," said Grove [*HBR*, Inside Intel,

N/D 1996].

By all odds, Intel should have been destroyed by international competition as had happened in other industries from tires to apparel, television to shoes. But Intel didn't fail. Grove posed a hypothetical question to his colleague Gordon Moore (of Moore's Law fame). "If we got kicked out and the board brought in a new CEO, what do you think he would do?" Moore answered without reluctance, "He would get us out of memories." To which Grove responded, nearly numb, "Why shouldn't you and I walk out the door, come back, and do it ourselves?" That's what they did — an outside-in perspective along with the courage to act on it. They fired and re-hired themselves to save their company. It wasn't easy. "To be completely honest about it, as I started to discuss the possibility of getting out of the memory chip business, I had a hard time getting the words out of my mouth without equivocation," admitted Grove. So they committed themselves to microprocessors, a much less developed business. The bold decision to commit Intel's future to microprocessors — a decision to break with the past and the gravitational pull of the familiar and the seemingly certain — saved the company and started it on the road to greatness. It wasn't a reasonable decision, but a reminder of the will to let go and do what is painful. [*HBR*, Inside Intel, N/D 1996]

Tough calls aren't always bet-the-farm or swing-for-the-fences with so much on the line. But the kind of decisions that keep us up at night — firing a rising star who isn't a cultural fit, breaking from protocol or process, nagging quality problems or customer service issues that are embarrassingly repeated — these tough calls are no less crucial. Legacy leaders unswervingly stick to their decision, stay with their plan even when things begin to crumble around them because they despise the thought of permanently turning back. They have a sustained, enduring devotion to finish. Their persistence is almost legendary. They feel a responsibility to make their small part of the world better than it was when they found it. They ask: "Now what needs to be done?"

When have you heeded the call to make a difficult, unpopular or contentious decision where something big was on the line? What is your "now what needs to be done" quest that makes your team's small part of the world better?

Resilient/Antifragile. Fragile things break under stress. According to Nassim Nicholas Taleb in *Antifragile*, there's an entire class of other things that don't simply resist stress, but actually grow, strengthen, improve from excessive stimuli. He has coined them antifragile. Resilient things bounce back. Antifragile things become better because adaptable systems can cope with exceeding stress and overcome inherent vulnerability without collapsing. Legacy torchbearers find purpose in trying circumstances. They use their adversity to help someone else unfamiliar with that adversity to not simply 'deal with it' but to grow from it.

What's the internal script that your team tells themselves in crisis, in failure, in desperation, in anxiety, in frustration, in hardship? That script isn't determined by their education or their talents or their profession; the script comes from leaders. Adversity awakens something inside us. It can unexpectedly arrive in numerous forms — mounting debt, a public crisis, plummeting market share, mass layoffs, death of a leader — and it's always unwelcome. Sometimes the riptide of tragedy and loss can pull us under and leave us gasping for air, far from shore, panicked. But adversity is an essential element of the torchbearer's narrative because it shows us how to grow and stretch and overcome; adversity lights a way for others.

When has adversity been a catalyst for positive change in you, your team, your organization so you weren't just resilient, but antifragile?

Walt Disney Betrayed

Walt Disney was on a train from Hollywood to New York anticipating that he was going to be making deal with his financial backer, Charles Mintz. Walt was asking for more money for his next animated film. He certainly had his doubters even after getting this far. Many disbelieved that people would pay to see an animated film, but in 1927, "Trolley Troubles," featuring Oswald the Rabbit, was a hit. What Walt didn't know was that Mintz was going behind his back to create his own studio — Charles Mintz Studios — and convinced nearly the entire Disney crew of animators to join him. When Walt arrived in New York, Mintz offered him the role of President of the new studio with a lucrative salary. But Walt balked and walked away essentially without a studio, without cartoonists and without a cartoon character, since Oswald was now owned by Mintz.

On the train back to Hollywood, stunned by the betrayal, financially tattered, terrified about starting over, and facing a slump of fresh ideas for a new character, Walt was destitute and despondent. But on that nearly weeklong train ride, Mickey

Mouse was born at the crossroads of tragic circumstances and the power of passionate persistence. To make Mickey's feature film, "Steamboat Willie," pioneering the use of sound in animation, Walt had to sell his car and re-mortgage his home. The little mouse with big ears and a squeaky voice was a smash hit, and a new cartoon was produced each month. Disney isn't just a remarkable company, it created an industry of animation and family entertainment, from the ashes of adversity.

Giant slayers. We don't always grow when we want to, we grow because the circumstances require it. The dragons and the giants we face — they make the heroes. When you remove the dragons, you lose the hero. People in dire, difficult situations respond in inspiring ways. Personal giants don't stop at the door of your work. Cancer is a giant. Divorce is a giant. Alzheimer's is a giant. Elder caregiving is a giant. Alcoholism is a giant. A prodigal child is a giant. Overcoming the inner critic is a giant. Holding down two jobs is a giant.

Professional giants loom large too. A plant shut-down is a giant. A product recall is a giant. A massive new industry competitor is a giant. Plummeting brand reputation and poor publicity are giants. A fire is a fiant. In 1995 Malden Mills, the company who invented the fabric Polartec, was devastated when a fire broke out, the largest fire in Massachusetts in over a century. It was one of the few employers in town. At a time when Enron was headlines and corporate executives were making fortunes for themselves while driving their companies into bankruptcy, costing employees their jobs and sometimes their life savings, Aaron Feuerstein made a decision that others in the plummeting textile industry found hard to believe – he decided to pay his employees for their full salaries for the next 60 days while the plant was rebuilt. "I was proud of the family business and I wanted to keep that alive, and I wanted that to survive. But I also felt the responsibility for all my employees, to take care of them, to give them jobs. I think it was a wise business decision, but that isn't why I did it. I did it because it was the right thing to do," says Feuerstein. (Leung, 2003)

What happens at the margin of our decision to climb, our

comeback, our turnaround?   Bravery, boldness, courage and conviction aren't inherently natural when we are facing fear in our lives.   But people in dire, desperate circumstances respond in inspiring ways when the hope of torchbearers light the way, when they have a legacy leader helping them to face their giants.

Legacy Story Starters

When have you seen boldness light the way at work?   Tell a defining moment story about a time when you or your team have come up taller in the face of adversity.   How did you grow from the experience?

Leaders carry the responsibility of determining what needs to be done toward an great ambition.   What is your artistry in getting people to do what needs to be done when the stakes are high but the path is dimly lit?

Tell a story about a time when you broke a paradigm or were a catalyst for change.   How did it change you and the organization?   What did you "become" from it?

CONNECTION

How do you touch people and connect with them personally?

Leadership is personal.   It's not mechanistic.   People follow people.   Your team wants to know you as a person.   Who influenced you, what drives you, what are your pet peeves and hot buttons, what gets you fired up, what you care deeply about, why do you love your work or your profession, what are your non-negotiables?   Authenticity forges connection through trust. People want to know that you are real, that you've made mistakes and learned from them, that you have a heart and aren't callous, that you are deeply passionate, that you act on principles when it comes at a cost.   They don't want to hear about your accomplishments and accolades.   They want to hear your stories

— the messy, imperfect stories that show you are human, that show you are like the rest of us.

In 2015, *Harvard Business Review* reported findings from a Harris poll of 1,000 U.S. employees about communication issues between leaders and their teams. Some of the top results included not having time to meet with employees, not recognizing employees achievements, refusing to talk to subordinates. Most of the responses represent an inability to bond and build a healthy relationship. The data shows that the vast majority of leaders are not engaging in crucial moments that could help employees see them as trustworthy (Solomon, 2015).

Legacy leaders lead people not numbers; they are statesmen. They treat employees more than fairly and justly; they treat them like family, like kin. They care not just about results, but about the people; they care about you. They care enough to teach you. They care enough to have your back when you mess up. They care enough to give you a second and third chance. They care by being a little tough on you, pushing you further then you could imagine. They care enough to give you time off to handle responsibilities, difficulties, and tensions at home.

Legacy leaders connect your employees' hearts with the heart of the company. One worker astutely said, "The ultimate purpose of company is from the Latin "cum panis" meaning with bread. The first companies on earth were merchants who would meet and discuss their business plans over dinner (with bread) and discussed how the work they do will impact the people around them. Legacy comes from helping a company go from beyond profit to bringing the best version of yourself and others."

Team members see these leaders' deep commitment and so commit. Workers see their leader's values and principles acted out, and so those principles seep into their lives. The best of a legacy leader brings out the best in the team, maybe even transforms the team. After some time, employees may find themselves following these leaders' behaviors and actions. I remember once receiving a handwritten note from a senior executive that boosted my confidence at a time when I sorely needed it. I could imagine him sitting in his office desk hand writing the note to me in the busyness of his jam-packed day. Since then personal, hand-written notes have become a common practice I use to express gratitude to my employees.

What people say about you will not be about what you achieved in business, but about what you achieved for others. People commit to people, not deliverables or targets. Studies have shown that social bonding drives high performance teams more than raw talent. To your direct reports, you are the most important leader in your organization. You are the person most likely to influence their performance, their mood when they arrive home, the energy they feel at work, the confidence they need to grow. One worker said it well explaining a legacy leader: "She connected beyond the task to find the common human bond."

Legacy leaders build healthy connections through personal relationships, growing people as individuals, and contributing to a community. Driven people have an unconscious propensity to underinvest in their families and overinvest in their careers. Legacy leaders connect through personal example how to balance the demands at work with the demands at home. They know that enduring happiness begins with loving relationships at home. They want their team members to be *life successful* — not rich professionally, but poor relationally. Do you have a sense of what home life is like for your team? Do you offer help with small acts of kindness?

Legacy Story Starters

Legacy leaders have heart. How do you find your heart? How do you touch people? How do you ensure that life at work and at home is an enduring source of happiness for your team?

Characteristics of Connection

The crisis of confidence in senior leaders is global and worsening. For nearly twenty years, the Edelman Trust Barometer has surveyed tens of thousands of people across numerous countries about their level of trust in government, media, business, and non-government organizations. In 2017, 63% of survey respondent said CEOs are not at all or only somewhat credible. Just 52% of respondents said they trust businesses to do what is right.

Your team members need to be committed, compelled, convinced. They need to trust you, connect with you, believe in you, confide in you. They need to be willing to be followers and declare you as their leader, not by position or hierarchy or compulsion, but by delegation, by *their* choice. More than creating value, we expect our leaders to have values. We need leaders who we connect with, who are trustworthy, who are authentic. We need leaders who have restraint in their behaviors, who don't put greed-at-all-costs above people; leaders who model ethics. Here are the characteristics of legacy leaders who practice connection:

Show up with Authenticity. When Jeff Bezos announced in 2018 that he was increasing the minimum wage to $15 for all full-time, part-time, seasonal and temporary employees across the US, he revealed why Amazon made the change. "We listened to our critics, thought hard about what we wanted to do, and decided we want to lead." Bezos, long defending Amazon's pay practices, took negative feedback and criticism made about unfair pay of entry-level workers and used it as a catalyst for change. Years earlier when the *New York Times* published a scathing story about how Amazon put company performance above worker well-being, Bezos sent out a memo to all Amazon employees directing employees to report any incident similar to those in the story: "Even if it's rare or isolated, our tolerance for any such lack of empathy needs to be zero," wrote Bezos in the internal memo.

Being vulnerable is an integral part of intensifying trust and a precursor to authenticity. Legacy leaders don't try to fake it through their weaknesses, their flaws, their regrets and their type-A tendencies. Through the process of revealing themselves, introducing the real them to the real you, not the public persona, not the larger-than-life stories, legacy leaders teach apprentices that mistakes are what you make of them and reveal the dark corners of misjudgments and wrong turns. One worker said, "They own who they are…one hundred percent genuine."

In *The Brilliance of Failure*, Chris Brickman, a senior executive across numerous companies, candidly self-discloses his flaws as a leader: "When I started my first job, I was desperately insecure, but I was also an expert at covering it up with bravado and cockiness. I had grown up as the second child of a demanding family, and I was desperate to prove myself and stand out. I wrestled with demons…I would make inappropriate statements to draw attention to myself; I would share information I should have held in confidence; I would slightly alter the facts to make stories and information sound better. All of these tactics were intended to draw attention to myself or to get people to like me or think better of me." We all have imperfections that we carry from our formative years and these can affect our behavior and relationships in the workplace. We must acknowledge our "demons" by becoming aware of them. Sharing them makes us more human and approachable to people and creates a culture of safety, candidness and truthfulness.

How do you want them to know you? Are you approachable and vulnerable about your mistakes and misjudgments?

Kindness, Generosity and Empathy. Gallup's well-researched Q12 is a set of twelve questions that has become one of the most powerful predictors of employee engagement. It is based on more than thirty years of in-depth behavioral economic research involving more than seventeen million employees. One of the most surprising findings came from questions ten: *Do you have a best friend at work?* Think about it, in the highly researched and perks-as-the-norm world of employee engagement, the squishiness and subtlety of deep friendship is highly predictive of employee and workgroup performance. Legacy leaders promote kindness, caring and empathy as a set of behaviors and actions that builds healthy relationships between peers, team members, and employees.

How do you promote kindness, caring, and empathy with your

teams and in your organization?

Fluid Recognition. A Gallup study found that when managers provide meaningful feedback to employees, those employees are more than three times more likely to be engaged. A ten year, ten-thousand person study in the US and Canada by OC Tanner Institute and HealthStream found that recognition and appreciation tops the list of things employees say they want most from their employers. In the same study, seventy-nine percent of employees who consider quitting their job cite lack of appreciation as one of the key reasons for leaving, and of the people with highest morale, ninety-four percent agree their managers are effective at recognizing them.

There is a misplaced notion that the sole driver of stress in the workplace is excessive responsibility. Sure, outsized effort or preposterous workloads create stress, but it's the imbalance of effort and reward which makes us feel anxious, unappreciated and maybe a little bitter. Legacy leaders offer praise and recognition with deep sincerity and specificity. Their gratitude is abundant, not scant. Their appreciation abounds in the moment not as an afterthought.

Before process checks and revealing results, some legacy leaders start their meetings with gratitude. *Does anyone have something or someone they are grateful for?* Not an around-the-table obligation, but voluntary, meaningful thanks. When teams notice in each other the extra hard work, when they recall how someone made their day or achieved something significant, that kind of gratitude and noticing connects people. Let your team express their gratitude to each other. Waiting for end-of-the-year public recognition misses too many small, personal moments that go unnoticed.

Are you frugal with your praise, compliments and recognition or are you sincere, timely, and specific when you recognize employees or peers? Do you tell your team and apprentices that you are proud of them? Do you provide opportunities and encouragement for your team to appreciate each other?

Coach the best from people. In a Quantum Workplace study, just 60% of people believe that their performance is more likely to improve if they meet with their managers to discuss performance more frequently than once per year. That's a massive difference from the perception of managers at 80%. In the same study, 85% of highly disengaged employees say they don't receive enough coaching from their boss.

Legacy leaders take the time to understand the unique strengths of their people. They don't assume the same capability levels; they adjust their playbook and game plan like an astute coach leveraging diverse capabilities across their team. They are mature enough to see the blind spots in people, listen intently, and then prompt and shape the right experiences to grow them. They see their teammates' strengths and hone these competencies with stretch assignments. They masterfully elevate their team by blending each individual's gifts into a cooperative, symbiotic group.

Results matter, but do you get the best from people by piling on more and seeing how they handle it, testing their performance only through pressure? Do you coach the best from them across a wide array of experiences?

A Cohesive Team that Elicits Belonging and Commitment. Building a cohesive team is a signature discipline of effective leaders. In *Good to Great*, Jim Collins identified a practice of exceptional companies: the ability to confront the brutal facts while maintaining unwavering faith that you will prevail despite difficulties. No team can afford to hold back, so legacy leaders create a culture where people weigh in so they buy in. When there is trust, conflict's purpose is to find truth – the truth about our customer experience, the truth about our losing market share, the truth about our delayed launches. Conflict without trust perpetuates cattiness. Conflict with trust perpetuates truth. At the end of conflict, people might disagree, but they need to commit.

When people feel like they belong, they are free to be themselves. Your team members feel unashamed of their quirky personalities and silly mannerisms. They are more willing to take risks — personally and professionally — when they feel safe. Legacy leaders create and nurture an identity of the team that overshadows the individual or the leader. Your team members feel proud to belong to a tribe.

James Webb at NASA

While the first astronauts in space garnered most of the public attention, the behind-the-scenes administration in NASA's Apollo program deserves perhaps the greatest accolades. Some have deemed it the largest and most technically daunting engineering enterprise ever undertaken in the modern age. James Webb was the NASA Administrator who orchestrated the Apollo program. Webb's greatest contribution was the "grand alliance" forged among government, industry, and academia toward a common purpose and team identity. A biography of Webb by NASA says, "Many believe that James Webb... did more for science than perhaps any other government official. The reason we got to the moon before the Russians was that they didn't have anybody to pull it together." In the end, the Apollo program would require the talents of nearly every community in the nation — spanning as many as 400,000 people at NASA, universities, and industry who worked on Apollo and the supporting scientific exploration programs. — under one vision and identity.

On Jan. 27, 1967, astronauts Virgil "Gus" Grissom, Edward White, and Roger Chaffee were killed during a test of the Apollo 1 capsule. Webb asked President Johnson to allow NASA to conduct its own examination, which it did, and then they presented the results of the investigation to the public. To stem any threat of the Apollo community identity linked to failure, Webb deflected much of the blame onto himself. "While he was personally tarred with the disaster, the space agency's image and popular support was largely undamaged," according to a NASA biography.

Relationships drive results. Legacy leaders solve by more collaboration, more connection, more trust and more synchronicity. Legacy leaders are granted permission by others to lead not based on organization charts with boxes and dotted lines. Legacy leaders are granted permission by others to lead not by being charismatic, but by being vulnerable. A leader who can't be vulnerable will destroy a team.

People have no idea what the challenges are of the leader when you are in the audience and locked into a limited point of view. Legacy leaders share the podium perspective with everyone in the audience. They see the world through the eyes of people. They care about team members as individuals, not as a means to drive numbers. They don't waste chances to be generous or miss opportunities to appreciate, nor are they meager in their compassion and empathy. Organizations take on the personality of the leader. Nurturing relationships just might be the final frontier in generating breakthrough performance.

Legacy Story Starters

When have you deeply connected with a colleague or leader? What were the "ingredients to the relationship stew?"

What is holding you back from deeply connecting with others, caring for them and empathizing with them? Is there something from your past or a false perception others have of you that might be holding you back?

How can you find ways to have others get to know you personally? Develop some story starters that reflect you as a person — your values, principles and convictions, your pet peeves and passions, your dreams and mistakes.

What are the most important relationships that shaped you?

CULTURE

What are the conditions that bring out the best in your team members?

Organizational success or failure is largely based on leadership excellence, not managerial expertise, shrewdness, or intelligence. People want more from their leaders. Employees can work for dozens of good-enough bosses and leaders in their lives. But legacy leaders create a culture that moves us, marks us, makes us. One worker said it shrewdly, "[Positive legacy leaders] create a 'school of thought' for learning...They innovate in organizational culture. They stand up against the norm of how things are done until it becomes the norm…not for themselves, but because they have the betterment of the organization or its people at the heart of what they do."

The conditions of work, the context of the work, the expectations of the leaders and the team creates a culture, and as Peter Drucker so famously stated, "Culture eats strategy for breakfast." Culture, more than processes and procedures, defines how things get done. Over time and under the right circumstances, the core values, norms, and convictions of a team or organization create a shared identity that has the power to shape us. One of the most important jobs of a leader is to create a positive, encouraging, result-oriented culture, a set of principles, philosophies, and behaviors that fosters unity, teamwork, appreciation, transparency, resolve, and hope. Legacy leaders create the working conditions for employees to flourish; they are culture cultivators. They build a unique habitat in their organizational ecosystem. They don't just accept the organizational culture as-is, but they are constantly shaping it, tinkering with ways-of-working improvements. They identify with the culture in a deeply personal way — a culture that reflects their personal values, a culture with a purpose that is meaningful to them, a culture that inspires people to give their best because they love the work.

Fake culture is a result of fake people. Customers will never love a company until employees love it first. Great cultures are places where people can express themselves honestly and be recognized and celebrated for their achievements. Legacy leaders understand that you get what you pursue. If you pursue accolades, momentary applause, amorphous praise, that's all you'll get. Results and relationships are more important to legacy leaders than being seen as smart, so they put their weaknesses on the table and truly expect others to do the same. As one worker said, "[Negative legacy leaders] promote their personal agendas over their team and they eventually end up very, very isolated, lonely, and without constituents."

Bad cultures breed bad leaders, and bad leaders breed bad

cultures. We are deeply affected by our work culture. The tone of the workplace is set by the leader. Legacy leaders know that performance can go up or down — vacillating not only due to effort, but sometimes due to luck or unforeseen circumstances. But great organizational cultures can always be relied on to stabilize against the storms; great cultures carry shared traditions that create a sense of responsibility and belonging to drive progress. Culture cultivators turn up the volume on mission because products can be similar, easily substitutable, but missions are unique. They drive a desire to change something for the better. Legacy leaders see culture, not their products or services, as the differentiator.

Where the leader goes, so goes the culture. Where the culture goes, so goes the company. Your culture matters more than you think. Culture is the multiplier of intelligence. Culture is the multiplier of performance. Culture is the multiplier of commitment and development. Legacy leaders understand that process alone won't get you where you need to go. Culture is paramount and culture drives results.

3M's 15% Culture

Decades before Google made 20%-time fashionable, 3M pioneered an overt culture of creativity and innovation in 1948 with its unique 15% Culture — encouraging employees to set aside a portion of their work time to proactively cultivate and pursue innovative ideas that excite them. Regardless of their assignment, 3M technical employees are encouraged to devote up to fifteen percent of their working hours (a little more than a half day per week) to independent projects. Employees are accountable to deliver their day-to-day responsibilities, but in coordination with their manager, they are provided enough margin and money to try something new – whether it's a new technology, a fresh idea based on a hunch or even experiment with a new process or framework. Employees are encouraged to challenge the status quo. "3M has a tolerance for tinkerers and a pattern of experimentation that led to our broadly based, diversified company today. To borrow a line from 'Finnian's Rainbow,' you might say we learned to 'follow the fellow who follows a dream,'" says Gordon Engdahl, retired vice president, Human Resources.

The 15 percent philosophy flies in the face of standard management ideas about control. The foundation of 3M's collaborative and organizational culture started with William McKnight, who served as the President and Chairman of the Board for 37 years (1929-1966). He was a visionary in his perspective on people and innovation: "Hire good people and leave them alone. As our business grows, it becomes increasingly necessary to delegate responsibility and to encourage men and women to exercise their initiative. Management that is destructively critical when mistakes are made kills initiative. And it's essential that we have many people with initiative if we are to continue to grow."

Freedom to explore independently – even if the boss says otherwise - has been part of the 3M culture for decades. "Bootlegging" was a time-honored practice. The early leaders of 3M understood that no one should stand in the way of a creative person with passion because that person might invent the next product or manufacturing breakthrough. This has paid off handsomely. Countless innovations have been created thanks to the 15% Culture – Scotch™ masking tape, Multilayer Optical Film, Cubitron™ Abrasive Grains, Emphaze™ AEX Hybrid Purifier, APC™ Flash-Free Adhesive and Post-It® Notes. In any given week, 3M launches on average 25 new products around the globe. "The 15 percent rule is unique to 3M. Most of the inventions that 3M depends upon today came out of that kind of individual initiative . . . You don't make a difference by just following orders." says Bill Coyne, retired senior vice president, Research and Development.

Characteristics of Culture Cultivators

The real way to become great is to join a great team. Culture has the power to shape our identity. For decades, sociologists have asserted that behaviors are contagious. Scientists are finding that healthy or unhealthy habits are significantly determined by family and friends. The Framingham Heart Study, commenced in 1948 by the National Heart Institute tracked fifteen thousand Framingham, Massachusetts residents and their descendants in a longest running longitudinal health study. Researchers found that the likelihood of becoming obese increased 57% if a friend was obese. The likelihood of smoking increased 36% if a friend smoked (likewise the likelihood of quitting increased 34% if a friend quit). Even happiness was found to be contagious — each happy friend boosted one's happiness by 9%. Over time, norms and values of the group to which we belong, under the right circumstances, become our own. We internalize them.

Here are some characteristics of legacy leaders that develop exceptional cultures:

A Culture of Shared Values and Purpose. Legacy leaders carry "a big why" around their work and projects — a constant reminder why they are doing something. Legacy leaders put the *why* at the center of everything — why should the customer care, why should the company invest, why should this be a top priority, why should we personally get excited and passionate? They consciously put *the why* before *the what* because you engage and enroll people's hearts with a big why, not a big what. The why is the big idea, the big vision, the big opportunity. The why is a meaningful mission.

Legacy leaders encourage people to see their work as a calling; what Amy Wrzesniewski, Professor of Organizational Behavior at Yale School of Management, calls job crafting – pushing the boundaries of a job in ways that make it more meaningful by finding purpose in the most mundane roles. Job crafters aren't handed such unconventional roles, but they are often self-made under the cultural encouragement of legacy leaders. Consider a nursing home caregiver. They can see themselves in the wearisome tasks of bathing and cleaning the sick and elderly or they can see their role as assisting in healing, encouraging patients during rehabilitation, buoying their spirits. (NPR How to build a better job. *Hidden Brain newscast,* 2016).

For the same exact job, work can mean different things under different workplace cultures. Some cultures restrict your job and others expand the contours of your job. Job crafters to some leaders could be seen as trouble makers breaking the rules. But to the legacy leader, they are the pioneers who go the extra mile, internalize the mission and go beyond their job description

Often executives spend too much time drafting, wordsmithing and redrafting visions statements, purpose statements, mission statements and a cornucopia of other statements, but they spend too little time aligning the values of the organization with operating behaviors. The founders of great, enduring companies like 3M, Hewlett-Packard and Johnson & Johnson didn't have a vision statement when they started. They usually began with a set of personal core values and a determination to embed them in their organizations. They didn't "set" their values but instead discovered them because they were predisposed to practicing them as part of a pursuing a purpose. Their principles emerged rather than being "founded."

Legacy leaders have a firm understanding of what they will or will not do not just based on strategy, but anchored in purpose and values. These values are usually revealed when the organization is under stress or at a crossroads. When you don't have mutually accepted, shared values, then things tend to become unhinged during stress. Legacy leaders adhere to their values even when exceptions are painfully difficult. The purpose of the organization or team is the lighthouse when the storms of doubt, difficult decisions or distress come rolling in.

Roy Vagelos and River Blindness

Twenty million people are affected by river blindness worldwide. The disease is spread by tiny blackflies that breed in streams. Like mosquitoes that transmit malaria, blackflies pick up a parasite and leave some larvae in humans when they bite. Within the human body the larvae becomes a tiny worm which then produces thousands of baby larvae which migrate to the skin and eyes. The death of these baby larvae is toxic, causing eye lesions which may lead to irreversible blindness. This is not just a scourge of human health but of economic development. Massive communities are abandoned around rivers where outbreaks occur. There are ghost towns in fertile valleys in Africa.

In 1978 a solution emerged in a Merck lab by research scientist William Campbell. Studying parasite worms for livestock and horses, Dr. Campbell saw a relationship between the variety of bacteria that kill the parasitic worms in horses (like the bacteria administered to dogs to treat heartworms) and the larvae in river blindness. The results were breathtaking in animals, but to study humans would cost millions over years with practically no promise of any economic value, since river blindness affected the most impoverished people on the planet. There was no prospect of paying customers. Does a company underwrite a product with no commercial value, even though it could lift a plague from the lives of millions of poor people?

In deciding whether to manufacture a drug that would never sell and likely cost more than $3 a tablet to produce and distribute, Roy Vagelos, CEO of Merck & Co. and one of the early scientists who developed the drug, made a bold commitment. Merck would give away the drug for free and even arrange for its distribution for as long as was needed in Africa. When scant resources were available for a global health policy, Vagelos made an unprecedented and nervy decision based on principle not profit.

At a press conference, Vagelos and other Merck officials described the "unique situation in which the drug was needed only by people who couldn't afford it...Sometimes in life, you've got to take a leadership position." African villagers walked all night to where they thought the drug would be dispensed. "An absolutely unforgettable moment of my professional life," said Campbell as he watched a snaking line of people waiting for the white tablets of Mectizan.

By 1997 the lost income from having given away the drug had reached two hundred million dollars — an investment equivalent to bringing a commercially viable product to market. Some, like Noble-prize winning economist Milton Friedman, call the actions, like Vagelos took, executive irresponsibility — spending shareholders money on anything but profitable ventures in the name of social responsibility. Vagelos once said, reflecting on Merck's mission, "We never try to forget that medicine is for the people not for the profits." *The New York Times* in 1992 wrote that Merck's development of Mectizan "will surely rank as one of the century's greatest medical triumphs."

Interestingly, the seeds of Vagelos's decision was built into Merck's DNA decades earlier. After World War 2, tuberculosis surged. In war-devastated Japan, few people could pay for a potent Merck drug, streptomycin, highly effective in treating this deadly disease. Coming at a moment of great hardship for Japan, Merck decided to donate a massive supply to the Japanese public.

Does your team understand why your organization exists? What are your core values that define how people should behave? When have your values been put to the test?

A Culture of Unity and Safety. Legacy leaders know how to nurture real teamwork, which is created when team members implicitly trust each other to deliver their part, to share information without restraint, and to listen deeply to diverse opinions. Culture cultivators create places where people aren't afraid to be themselves. They don't waste time pretending — faking vulnerabilities and phantom performance — but rather express themselves and their work honestly. Legacy leaders make their team feel safe so cooperation is an unhindered expectation and trust allows for healthy debate. Grandstanding and finger-pointing isn't tolerated. Hiding mistakes is shunned because it dampens learning for all. People don't worry about pleasing others through politics.

Legacy leaders believe that none of us is as smart as all of us. They understand that the more connected workers are, the safer they feel, the more committed they are. If people feel safe with each other, then they push each other not to climb the ladder or strive for personal gain, but to advance the work of the team. They don't fear repercussions from their colleagues when they take missteps, but rather they receive grace and forgiveness, encouragement and extra hands to help. On a team led by a legacy leader no one waits to watch someone eventually fall.

Great teams celebrate each other's success and don't resent it. They require deep collaboration where they leverage everyone's strengths — beyond role and responsibility — for the good of the team. Great teams self-assemble in ways to compensate for weaknesses, and are willing to be selfless for an individual's development opportunities.

We cannot force people to trust us, to innovate for us, to collaborate with each other for the sake of the team. Those actions are the result when people feel safe. We cannot tell people to commit —they are committed because they want to be, committed because they care enough about each other. They know their leader and everyone else has their back.

How can you elevate the safety your team feels at work? Do you have a culture of "in it together," a culture that promises, "if one of us fails, then all of us fail"? Does your team celebrate success of individuals without envy? Does your team self-assemble in ways to deliver the best result?

A Culture of Twenty-Mile Marches. Roald Amundsen and Robert F. Scott, a Norwegian and a Brit, both set out for the South Pole to claim it first. Only one of them returned. They started their expeditions within a month of each other. Both were accomplished in their own right, well-resourced and trained. Both actually reached the South Pole, Amundsen first. But Scott and his team that journeyed to the South Pole never returned. When historians forensically assessed the diaries of the expeditions, they found Scott had vacillated in the daily treks — inclement weather might cause them to camp for days under blizzard-like conditions, then push excessively to exhaustion on fair weather days. Amundsen, by contrast, would trek approximately twenty miles every day. That was the plan he conjured thousands of miles away after months of planning, and that was the plan he doggedly executed. No matter what weather they faced, no matter how tired they were — twenty miles. Practically never more and never less. Twenty miles every day, each day. Incredible persistence.

Undaunted pursuit. A clear and focused plan executed despite the conditions around him.

Here's a different twenty mile march. A march of character. A march of delivering on a commitment. This isn't the twenty mile march of explorers vying for fame but of everyday people, hidden leaders in our workplaces, who set an example for all of us. Enter Walter Carr, the Birmingham, Alabama college student who walked twenty miles through the night when his car broke down, rather than miss his first day of work at a moving company.

The 20 Mile March is more than a philosophy. It's having clear performance mechanisms that keep you on track. The rigor creates two types of self-imposed discomfort: the discomfort of unwavering commitment to high performance in difficult conditions; the discomfort of holding back in good conditions. But these discomforts create an advantage by building confidence to perform in adverse circumstances and exert self-control in highly favorable circumstances.

Walter Carr's 20 Mile March

Walter Carr had jobs in the past as a cook at fast-food restaurants, but a moving company job paid better, and he needed the money to pay the rent on an apartment he'd recently rented. After friends said they couldn't give him a ride to work, rather than miss his first day of work, he "went out walking." According to the route on Google Maps, it was about twenty miles and it would take him about eight hours. Carr ate a meal of bologna and eggs at eight p.m. and then took a nap at home before his journey. At midnight, he woke up, grabbed his wallet, phone, and a baseball bat to protect him from stray dogs. He headed out into the dead of night just to get to work on time. Carr ascribes his grittiness to his mom, who'd often said, "Nothing is impossible unless you say it's impossible."

He choose the hard path when nobody was watching. His decision was made of pure character, pure heart. In an age when small inconveniences rile us, in an age when people give up because the opposition seems too difficult, Carr is an example of doing hard things when something important is on the line, when you need to close the gap between where you are and where you want to be.

There's more to the story. Police officers picked him up and bought him breakfast because he had no cash, then drove him to the home where he was moving a family. The moving company CEO was so moved by Walter's commitment and example that he gave him his car. Walter is no CEO, but his leadership is exemplary and he represents the scores of people in our teams who are doing the impossible, closing the gap in their lives at home and work.

There's often more on the line than you think. That line is different for all of us, but nonetheless, the line matters because it calls forth something in each of us. To pusher harder — not to the brink, but to the edge, to find a way. Not to stop when it's hard, but to discover that when it's hard, we learn the most about ourselves and we create a culture that sticks to its commitments.

In *Grit*, Angela Duckworth describes how grit is a preeminent determinant of success — far exceeding talent and genius. From West Point to Spelling Bees, from employees at JPMorgan Chase to Olympic athletes, from genius studies from the 1920s to present-day treadmill tests, Duckworth explains how passion to accomplish a goal combined with sustained, enduring devotion and perseverance to follow-through in the face of life's rejection are core determinants of grit. "Enthusiasm is common. Endurance is rare," says Duckworth. Sure, grit sparks from an inner drive, but the culture in which we work and with which we identify powerfully shapes us. Gritty cultures create gritty team members. Gritty cultures are formed from gritty leaders. They set the tone. And often they do it habitually every day — they begin each day setting the culture. They have rituals and artifacts that reinforce their culture.

Tell the Truth Mondays

Pete Carroll, head coach of the Seattle Seahawks, instills a culture of continuous improvement in his teams. One way Carroll encourages this kind of learning intensity is with a film review of games. "Tell-The-Truth Monday" is when game mistakes are corrected, big plays praised together as a team. All of it; full transparency. It's a deliberate approach to discuss what happened in the game and to be honest with each team member's performance.

Duckworth equates achievement to talent, skill and effort, but effort counts twice:

Talent x Effort = Skill

Skill x Effort = Achievement

Effort builds skill and effort makes skill productive. Without effort, talent is just unfulfilled potential. Without effort, skill is what you could have done but didn't. When you quit, effort goes to zero. Legacy leaders create cultures with stamina, firmness, fierce resolve, courage, endurance, and determination. They know that effort comes from the aggregation of small improvements at the edge of one's ability practiced daily. When teams experience the inner satisfaction that comes from doing something important and doing it with rigor — doing it even though it's hard — they want more of it. Allegiance to high standards raises the potential of everyone around them.

How will you create a culture of grit that has staying power — one that is reinforced and expressed in daily rituals?

Mutual Accountability and Intent-based Leadership. Legacy leaders know that the primary source of accountability is with peers not the boss. The best teams don't rely on the boss for accountability, but themselves. They hold each other accountable for the right behaviors, because behaviors precede results.

Legacy leaders encourage straightforwardness — candid conversations and transparency. Their teams acknowledge problems and move on and thereby squash the fear of admitting weakness. Constructive conflict and respectful debate are common to drive sound decisions. They don't sweep conflict under the rug but favor passionate debate over peace because it brings out the best solutions. They pull people together without the rivalries which often shatter connectedness. They are hard on the problem, fair to the people.

In his book, *The Difference*, Subir Chowdhury asks a telling, metaphorical question: *What do you do if you see a toothpick on the floor?* When you see something that doesn't belong or is misplaced or just isn't right — what do you do? Scores of companies have cultures where people sweep problems under the rug, even in front of their bosses, hiding behind an "it isn't my job" mindset or fearful to expose the truth. Fear eventually creates a mindset of indifference at best and lying at worst.

Culture cultivators build mutual accountability into the work of their teams. Not only do they set high expectations to deliver results, but they create an environment where the team holds each other accountable. Candor and clarity lead to accountability. Collaborative problem-solving shoves individual rights and wrongs to the side and propels the goal beyond individual interests. Team members help each other be right, not wrong. They assume positive intent. They don't create negative assumptions about each other but help each other win and take pride in each other's victories as shared successes.

Legacy teams delicately balance unwavering determination with personal humility. Team members are willing to put their weaknesses on the table, admit mistakes because delivering results is more important than being seen as smart. When someone is aware of something that needs to be done, they choose to act with resolve not cogitate on whose responsibility it neatly falls under. They carry the tacit obligation to stand up for the right thing to do together. They are provided the freedom, autonomy, and trust to do the right thing.

Captain David Marquet Takes the *Santa Fe* from Worst to First

In 1998, U.S. Navy Captain David Marquet was assigned to be the captain of *USS Santa Fe* (SSN-763), a nuclear-powered submarine. At the time, the *Santa Fe* was one of the poorest performing, lowest-scoring submarines in the Navy — excessively high attrition rates coupled with unacceptable performance evaluations made his job steep. When David noticed his crew taking direct orders from him despite his commands being wrong, he realized that his crew would do anything he ordered in the typical leader-follower mindset — even if it was wrong. That could be catastrophic. So he decided to try intent-based leadership, what he calls "a leader-leader approach," counter to his training in the Navy.

Captain Marquet began treating his crew as leaders, not followers. He enabled and empowered his crew so they were proactive, responsible and accountable, ultimately sharing control with them. In the leader-leader model each person is thought of, and thinks of himself or herself, as a leader. So instead of "requesting permission" to do something, David taught his crew to take a proactive, thoughtful stance by stating "I intend to..." which moved them from passive followers doing what they were told to engaged leaders. David's responsibility changed too from control to choice: to trust his crew to get on with a recommendation, to provide support behind a recommendation, or to suggest an alternative course of action. Mutual accountability not just "accountable at the top" permeated down the organization. As he slowly moved the commander's intent down the ladder, David's crew showed initiative and innovative thinking. The *Santa Fe* went from "worst to first," achieving the highest retention and operational standings in the Navy.

Does your team care deeply enough to make a difference with unwavering determination and pride in the outcomes, or are they simply checking the boxes? Do they understand what must be done and muster the resources to pursue it proactively? Do they "request permission" or suggest innovative recommendations? Do they hold each other to high standards for the collective good?

A Culture of Ownership. Legacy leaders create a culture of ownership so employees feel and act like owners. They have a deep devotion, almost reverence, to the legacy of the company. They have a sense of history and their place in the future of the organization so their teams feel part of the purpose — "this is who we are." In the Gallup 2013 State of the Workforce poll, less than fifteen percent of people reported feeling an emotional connection or engagement with the company they worked for.

Team members need to know how they are contributing to a bigger vision and story, so legacy leaders create a North Star and point their team toward it. Culture cultivators know that if you want people to act, they must feel. They must develop an unrelenting pursuit of something meaningful, something that matters. Despite the obstacles, circumstances, and set-backs, they know that this is where we are going. This is the virtual place people gather. Everyone aspires to be part of something bigger than themselves.

Hamdi Ulukaya at Chobani

With no prior experience Chobani founder, Hamdi Ulukaya, has created a billion dollar yogurt empire. The Chobani story isn't just about revolutionizing yogurt. It's also about revitalizing once economically depressed communities from rural communities in places like upstate New York and Twin Falls, Idaho, by creating a deep connection with employees. Hamdi purchased a shuttered yogurt factory in South Edmeston, New York, from Kraft. The closure was a blow to the small town. But through a deeply rooted connection to former employees and citizens, Ulukaya built his start-up using former employees; Chobani grew and prospered. The company now employs more than two thousand workers. Ulukaya chooses to pay minimum wages that are beyond the government limit. He pays his workers handsomely and also rewards them with an equity stake in the success and prosperity of Chobani. "This isn't a gift," he explains. "It's a mutual promise to work together with a shared purpose and responsibility."

Culture cultivators create an intense environment that requires people to bring their best, a work environment that is both totally exhausting and totally exhilarating, a work environment where people are able to utilize their full abilities and capabilities, stretching themselves and their colleagues to become better. They pull the best out of people by asking, *"Is this your best?"* A culture like that is not driven by fear — *do I measure up? Am I good enough?* — but by a drive to reach its full potential. If you are a legacy leader, when your work is done, your people will look at the accomplishment and say proudly, "We did this." Legacy leaders expect their teams to succeed on their own merits. They don't feel the organization owes them anything. One worker said it this way, "I'll never forget my favorite boss. Not because he was affable, likable and let me do my work, but because he got things from me I didn't know I had to give. He set expectations that seemed insurmountable, but he gave us three things: a why, hope, and his dedication. I would do almost anything not to disappoint him. I learned more about myself in those two years than in the ten prior. I grew like weed under him. He was nurturing my career, not in a paternalistic, pandering way, but in a "tough love" kind of way."

How can you create an environment of intense ownership? How can you reframe your work so your team feels part of something bigger? How will you create an environment where people have a gigantic opportunity to make a difference?

A Clear Vision and Tight Focus. Most visions don't have much staying power or longevity without significant focus. Most visions just don't have much stickiness. When we are consumed with the present, the larger vision can take a backseat. Adherence to the longer term, to the ethereal, seems a luxury when the demands of today feel like they are threatening the business. Complexity can make the vision less sticky. Time has a way of eroding the glue of vision unless the glue is reapplied. Culture cultivators keep the vision at the forefront; they are constantly reapplying the glue.

Sure, failure can derail the vision journey, but less obvious and perhaps more common is how success can lure us into taking our hands off the wheel. Nothing can create failure quite like success.

Here's an all-too-typical scenario: An organization attains heathy success vs. its competition. Its reputation in the industry soars. Believing that everything is and will continue to be great, complacency sets in, which undermines the feisty continuous improvement mindset necessary for growth. Mediocrity sets in like atrophied muscles. In the worst case, the company completely loses sight of its vision. Often, leaders over-correct by "fixing" things, but the fixing doesn't work when there's an overemphasis on burn-the-furniture cost cutting.

It's easy to see turnarounds as exercises in simply improving the numbers. Declining sales, slumping profit margins, negative cash flow, and falling market share are only symptoms to the problem. The only way to fundamentally restore what is broken — not simply to temporary patch it up — is to become better by restoring the culture with a recommitment to its values and vision.

Alan Mulally at Ford

When Alan Mulally was named president and CEO of Ford in 2006, the famous American automaker was on the brink of bankruptcy. The company was preparing to post the biggest annual loss in its 103-year history—$12.7 billion. Seven years later, Mulally was widely credited with one of the most impressive corporate turnarounds in history. He guided Ford out of billions in losses, avoided bankruptcy without government bailouts, and starting winning back significant market share.

Paramount to the turnaround has been the creation of a new company culture. Alan created positive leadership as a principle for his management team — conveying the idea that there is always a way forward; there is always a way to figure out how to move a team, a project, or an initiative ahead. He created a culture of team work and accountability, reinforcing the idea that everyone is essential and everyone needs to be included. He created a vision that became known as "One Ford."

"One Ford" means everyone is part of the team and everyone's contribution is respected. To underscore the dramatic change this represents, think about a typical circumstance when an employee decides to stop the production line. As Mulally describes it, "In the past at Ford, someone would have jumped all over them: 'What are you doing? How did this happen?' It is actually much more productive to say, 'What can we do to help you out?' Because if you have consistency of purpose across your entire organization and you have nurtured an environment in which people want to help each other succeed, the problem will be fixed quickly. So, it is important to create a safe environment for people to have an honest dialogue, especially when things go wrong."

Measured Scale through Self-Discipline. Companies that scale well are self-disciplined; they have sacred constraints and principles that can never be compromised. Scaling isn't only about getting bigger; it's also about getting better — spreading exceptional ideas, ways of working, business models. Sutton and Rao in *Scaling Up Excellence,* say it best, "When people think growth, usually they think of anatomy. How big are the limbs? But the real thing is physiology. Is stuff circulating well — the blood and the oxygen? Even if your anatomy is very developed, your physiology can be bad." When management, efficiency and standardization eclipse attenuation to values and water down the right customer experience, then the sensibility of those decisions needs to be questioned. Cultures that scale well know that it isn't just about expanding the footprint, but extending the mindset — the deeply engrained beliefs, principles and behaviors that get injected in everything from the architectural design to service delivery to hiring practices and employee on-boarding [How to Grow without losing what makes you great, *Inc.,* Leigh Buchanan].

La Colombe's Attenuation to Core Principles

Todd Carmichael and JP Iberti, self-described coffee-geeks, founded La Colombe on a simple but profound passion: America deserves better coffee. Todd says, "Coffee is a brown fluid. It was treated in restaurants like salt, sugar, napkins — nothing special about it. And I knew there was something special about it. It was a commodity, it didn't have a face, it didn't have a name. It was just there on the table. Coffee at the end of meals can be quite disappointing, and I wanted to change that." Todd borrowed on the traditions of sourcing and roasting coffee from Europe and set out to create a "culinary coffee" to be enjoyed at upscale restaurants after a great meal. Today, La Colombe Coffee Roasters has 750 employees and runs twenty-six cafés in five cities, distributing its coffee to some 3,500 restaurants, hotels, cafés and retailers.

There are plans to open nearly a hundred more cafes throughout the U.S. within the next five years, but scaling the brand is more important than the growth numbers to Todd. Todd expresses his passion for great coffee, great conversation and connection through his branded cafes; coffee is handcrafted and he wants people to see how La Colombe employees work with their hands. "If [people] want to transcend from life for a few minutes...from all the worries throughout the day...if they could disconnect and be a little bit happier than our goal has been met. We move a lot of people in and out of our cafes, but we can still have a real conversation and make eye contact. I always tell our employees, who are so important to the success of our cafes that it all comes down to this idea of making great interactions. I'm not talking about the financial transaction, I am talking about the interaction when the barista hands the person their drink. The ritual of having someone make you a coffee is really deep. We want people to spend time at the [coffee] bar so we can...make their drink better for them. We don't send people to the 'sugar island,' or 'shame island' where they go to pour their sugar in an untidy area where garbage is overflowing, and sugar is everywhere. The moment when the customer goes to pour their cream or sugar, that's a moment for us to connect with them, so we keep that process right at the bar with us." (Brin, 2017)

Contagious Positivity and Word Fasting. We are not positive because life is easy. We are positive because life can be hard and we need something and someone to lean on. Positive leaders create an environment where the future is waiting to be created. Culture cultivators understand that emotions and feelings are contagious. They understand their team is just as likely to catch their mood as a cold, so they are conscious of walking into a meeting and being either a germ or a big dose of vitamin C. Legacy leaders aren't delusional in the face of real business concerns. Candor and authenticity are paramount, but how you approach circumstances — with hope or despair, with can-do or likely-to-fail — matters on the margin.

Even under cruel adversity, legacy leaders look for the positives. In 1914, Thomas Edison's factory in West Orange, New Jersey, was virtually destroyed by fire. Although the damage exceeded two million dollars, the buildings were insured for only $238,000 because they were made of concrete and were thought to be fireproof. Much of Edison's life work went up in smoke and flames that December night. At the height of the fire, Edison's twenty-four year-old son, Charles, searched frantically for his father. He finally found him, calmly watching the fire, his face glowing in the reflection, his white hair blowing in the wind. The next morning, Edison looked at the ruins and said, "There is great value in disaster. All our mistakes are burned up. Thank God we can start anew." Three weeks after the fire, Edison managed to deliver the first phonograph (Clemmer, 1999).

The world trains people to be pessimistic. Cynicism and criticism are rampant in offices, breakrooms, and meetings. Complaining that "management isn't _____" or "co-workers can't _____," is stifling. Negativity suffocates individuals of the oxygen they need to be creative, act autonomously, and feel like they can succeed amid difficulties. Leadership is a transfer of belief, and belief — hope — is contagious. There is a growing body of evidence that optimism may be hardwired into the human body by evolution. Studies from cancer patients to heart-disease patients find that survival rates are significantly higher for optimists compared to non-optimists. If we expect people to fail, they probably will.

Hopefulness changes your brain by pumping chemicals that block pain and accelerate healing. Hope initiates the release of beneficial neurochemicals called endorphins and enkephalins. Hope is as vital to the brain as oxygen is to the air we breathe. Without hope, experiments might never have sparked an innovation, new businesses might never have started, social movements might never have rallied for justice.

I'm adamantly opposed to animal testing, but I have to share a study that illuminates the power of hope. In the 1950s, a Harvard-trained researcher based out of Johns Hopkins named Curt Richter ran some fascinating experiments on rats. He wanted to see how long rats could swim in two different conditions. In the first condition, he simply let them swim as long as they could before giving up. They lasted fifteen minutes. Then, in the other condition, right before they were about to reach their maximum threshold of fifteen minutes, he picked them up and dried them off and let them rest briefly before putting them back in. Guess how long they were able to swim after that? Another 15 minutes? Try sixty hours! After being saved those little rats swam for an absolutely astonishing 240 times longer. How is that possible? Richter said it was because of one very simple thing: hope. The rats believed there was a chance to survive so they just kept going.

Behaviors and attitudes of your organization or team's culture is infectious. Researchers have studied the tendency for people to unconsciously mimic the emotional expressions and feelings of others by simple exposure to them in what scientists call an emotional contagion (Carter, 2012). We are vulnerable to "catching" other people's emotions. Psychologists at Harvard University concluded in one study that "negative emotions are like the flu" — they spread. Another study found that rudeness, bad mood and hostility propagates others to behave similarly (Delgado 2018). Tony Schwartz, CEO of The Energy Project, says "Leaders, by virtue of their authority, exert a disproportionate impact on the mood of those they supervise."

Legacy leaders spread optimism. Optimists imagine a positive future and create positive expectations. Positive expectations can create a learning environment. Cognitive neuroscientist Sara Bengtson devised an experiment where she manipulated the positive and negative expectations of students while their brains were scanned and then observed how they performed on cognitive tests. The students who were primed to be optimistic with words such as "smart," "intelligent," "clever" scored better. She also observed how the brain processed mistakes. The brains of the negatively and positively primed students were remarkably different. The area of the brain that is involved in self-reflection and recollection (prefrontal cortex) was inactive in students who were primed with negative thoughts. After they made a mistake, their brains did not show signs of surprise. It was almost as if they'd expected to make the error. But those students primed with positivity had heightened activity; their brain signaling for them to take notice, to pay attention, to reflect on a mistake, to learn from it.

Legacy leaders are conscious of how their words set the cultural tone of a group. They are deeply aware of the power of positive words and equally sensitive to the power of *fasting* words or not speaking negative words. In *The Forty-Day Word Fast*, Tim Cameron introduces the provocative idea of eliminating the following types of words: judgements, criticism, sarcasm, negativity, complaining, and gossip. Cameron depicts his experience as a teacher and school administrator in the wake of negative, critical words — kids' confidence is shattered. Flippant critical remarks erode self-esteem. Legacy leaders do not accept the toxic verbal culture that discourages, disrespects and destroys collaboration. They are intentional not only about the words said – positive and encouraging – but also of the words not said – negative, critical, judging.

What is the hope and optimism your team feels today? How balanced are you in your positivity-to-negativity ratio? How balanced is the words from your team? Do you or your team need to word fast?

Ernest Shackelton's Lifesaving Leadership

"MEN WANTED: FOR HAZARDOUS JOURNEY. SMALL WAGES, BITTER COLD, LONG MONTHS OF COMPLETE DARKNESS, CONSTANT DANGER, SAFE RETURN DOUBTFUL. HONOUR AND RECOGNITION IN CASE OF SUCCESS. SIR ERNEST SHACKLETON"

Who would answer such an ad, which Shackleton placed in a London newspaper seeking recruits for his 1914 Imperial Trans-Antarctic Expedition?

In 1914, twenty-eight men set out on their ship, the *Endurance*, to be the first to cross Antarctica from one coast to the other via the South Pole. They headed out from a whaling outpost on South Georgia Island, despite warnings of pack ice — an expanse of large pieces of floating ice driven together into a nearly continuous mass. Within a month, the *Endurance* was frozen solid in ice with Antarctica in sight! But the moving ice carried them off course and farther away from land – sixty miles from continental Antarctica. Ten months later the *Endurance* was irreparably damaged, crushed by massive sheets of floating pack ice. Ernest Shackleton's Trans-Antarctica expedition of 1914 -1917 was one of the most incredible adventure stories of all time.

Nothing could prepare Shackleton and his men for their peril. Shackleton and his crew abandoned their ship and inhabited a piece of moving ice. After 634 days, including two winters in Antarctica, where temperatures can drop to -100 degrees F, the entire crew reached safety. Their courage was epic. Under less perilous circumstances, other expeditions folded under duress, hardship, and tension. Shackleton shows us that leaders facing change, sometimes tectonic change that requires abandoning a hard fought, deeply committed goal, may need to pivot to another goal. In this case, Shackleton scrapped the Antarctica dream, and every man's survival became his new goal.

The crew culture forged by Shackleton — the expectations each crew member had of each other, the hopeful morale, the optimism assumed — allowed them to prevail. He refused to let negativity set in. He kept his crew upbeat and hopeful for days, weeks, months, with no contact to the outside world. Shackleton was attentive to small details, because he knew that they mattered immensely when strung together over countless hours. For example, he left many supplies on the *Endurance* — microscopes and specimen collection devices — but saved a crew member's banjo. Long dark days with barely any daylight and nothing to do, in order to fight the mind-numbing boredom, the crew read poetry, performed skits, sang songs and played the banjo.

His crew trusted him, believed in him, followed him despite his imperfections (like his several attempts to reach land by dragging the lifeboat across the ice expanse looking for water). Because they felt his care for their safety, they knew he would not fail them. Even when the crew separated to trek the jagged peaks of Elephant Island looking for whalers, no one doubted Shackleton's fierce determination to return to save the sick and injured.

"He is an interesting kind of touchstone of what constitutes success, what really matters when the old bedrock seems to be on shaky ground. Good leaders do that. They provide some context to measure our worth and our endeavors by. They frame a moment to say 'here is what constitutes a good end,'" said Professor Nancy Koehn, Harvard Business School Professor of Business Administration.

When your team, your organization faces the abyss, how will you lead them? When your team or your organization gets massively disoriented or thrown way off-course, how will you find your hope and optimism to persist?

Shared Struggles. The circumstances and events that happen to you aren't meant to define you. You are meant to define the circumstances. Culture cultivators don't allow against-the-odds circumstances to negatively manipulate the state of mind of their teams. They look for ways to make ideas work, not for reasons they won't. Struggles aren't avoided but embraced. Shared struggles can be rites of passage for individuals and teams. Legacy leaders know that it's in the struggle that people grow, teams bond, and relationships are forged. Resilient, determined, persevering teams outperform even the most talented teams. Legacy leaders are willing to fail, and they don't give up after failing. They see failure as an opportunity to improve.

How can you use shared struggles to intentionally forge resilience, growth, and bonding in your teams?

Continuous Learning and Growth Mindset. Legacy leaders create a culture that thirsts for learning, for trying, for iterating, for experimenting. According to Carol Dweck, author of *Mindset* and professor of psychology at Stanford University, there are two types of mindsets: a fixed mindset and a growth mindset. In a fixed mindset, people believe their talent traits are fixed and cannot change; you are born with a certain amount and that's all you have. They see intelligence as fixed, talent fixed, strengths fixed, weakness fixed. So working to improve them isn't a focus. Talent leads to success...you either have it or you don't. In a growth mindset, people believe that talent and intelligence can grow with experience and learning. They believe people can get smarter through effort.

Legacy leaders create a culture of growth and learning by believing that basic abilities are the starting point for the potential of a team. They see learning as an essential path toward achieving results. The team can become smarter not just through acquiring new talented members, but by developing the collective intelligence of the team. Legacy leaders experiment and learn at the edges of their disciplines. They institutionalize learning. Employees walk away from teams as more astute practitioners, more capable professionals, trailblazers in their fields of expertise.

For legacy leaders, continuous improvement is cultish because they understand the power of compounding. When Dave Brailsford stepped in as General Manager and Performance Director of the British Cycling in 2010 he boldly said what no one was willing to say out loud — no British cyclist had ever won the Tour de France. Dave believed in something called the aggregation of marginal gains — he found 1% improvements in everything his team did. Tiny areas of improvement overlooked by almost everyone else. When aggregated together, tiny insignificant improvements compounding repeatedly can yield extraordinary results. When they found the best pillow or mattress for sleeping, they placed it in every hotel stay. From the ergonomics of the bike seat, to how they washed their hands to avoid infection, to weight of the tires, to texture of the shirt — countless tiny optimizations every day for months over an entire team. Tiny benefits accumulated over time across an entire team yielded massive gains. It made a difference and Team Sky didn't win the Tour de France in the 5 years they wanted, but they did it in 3 years.

What are the tiny gains that by themselves are miniscule but with diligence and consistency could be accumulated by your team or organization to yield dramatic results?

STORY

At the turn of the twentieth century, some French children made an incredible discovery in the Pyrenees Mountains — drawings of extinct animals in caves. The 35,000-year-old paintings on the walls of the Lascaux Caves are our earliest recorded evidence of storytelling. Stories brought the vividness of events to those who did not participate in the hunt, the flood, the great migration, the voyage. Storytelling has been used by companies and clans, families and teams, nonprofits and governments, across the world for thousands of years. Anthropologists tell us that one determinant of flourishing, enduring societies vs. ephemeral ones is the ability to transfer wisdom, lessons, and knowledge from one generation to the next. Cultures that have lasted for thousands of years pass the rules for what is expected from one generation to the next. In some African cultures, stories are so integral to the people that every question is answered by a story.

Storytelling is one of the most unifying elements of humanity. When we invented stories, we celebrated ordinary men and women doing incredible acts of surpassing kindness, boundless bravery, relentless love, unwavering character. It's how we learn, instill morals and values, and connect with one another, which makes it not just a powerful communication vehicle, but also a sociological tool. The skills we build with stories are transferrable to others.

From an evolutionary perspective, stories increase our chances of survival. You are able to process eleven million bits of information per second through your subconscious mind, but only forty bits per second using your conscious mind. We think less than we think we think. We react, spontaneously, effortlessly, with emotion and senses, using the past embedded in our memory as our guide. Our subconscious brain is instantly aware of what matters and what doesn't, instantly aware of what's dangerous and what isn't, instantly aware of what needs our attention and what doesn't. Because we are predominantly driven by survival, the subconscious knows we don't have time to think, so it makes immediate decisions, snap judgements, contextual perceptions based on ancient scripts from our past — stories, experiences, memories.

Stories are foundational.

When you ask employees to provide an example of leaving a legacy at work, they tell a story. Sometimes the story is recalled first-hand, and other times, the stories have been passed down from generations of experiences and lessons. Stories are the language of legacy at work. Apprenticing, Boldness, Connection and Culture are the foundation for building a legacy, but they come to life through story; they are imprinted into the fabric of organizations through stories. The death of legacy in business is when we stop telling stories.

Business is hungry for storytelling. Storytelling is the root for senior leaders to nourish next-generation leaders. If you want those around you and behind you to pick up where you left off – to finish the great unfinished work of your organization's transformation, then you need a story. If you want new employees to believe in the values that your organization holds so closely, then you need a story. If you want your team to act boldly, to forge with an intrepid spirit of discovery, then you need a story. If you want your mentee to get unstuck, to see their development gaps with fresh eyes, to second-guess their behaviors, then you need a story.

Stories have the transcendent power to break down barriers between leaders and their teams, between generations, between hierarchal organization charts with boxes and lines. People from different cultures and backgrounds connect through stories because stories allow people to relate to each other. Some leaders see their companies largely as recipients of fortunate or misfortunate industry conditions, victims of past management snafus or victors of celebratory successes. Other leaders see their companies as grand stories with their teams playing an active role in developing a sweeping narrative. These are the legacy leaders.

Jeff Bezos, founder and CEO of Amazon, banned PowerPoint presentations in executive meetings. What did he replace it with? A narrative. Executives sit silently for about thirty minutes to "read a six-page memo that's narratively structured with real sentences, topic sentences, verbs and nouns." We process in narrative, we talk in narrative, we recall in narrative. Story is the best way to transfer an idea to another person. The brain isn't wired to retain information that's structured as bullets on a slide. "We read those memos, silently, during the meeting," says Bezos. "It's like a study hall. Everybody sits around the table, and we read silently, for usually about half an hour...and then we discuss it."

Our brains are wired for story.
Storytelling is a key tool for leaders. When someone steps into an MRI machine, what we see while the brain listens to a story, is quite interesting. We don't see a bystander, but instead we see a participant. We see a mimicking of the storyteller's brain to the listener's brain. We see them coupled. Emotions are mirrored between the teller and the listener. The listener's brain connects to the teller's brain. Even the best decks with the most beautiful graphics can't do that. Stories do.

Princeton neuroscientist Uri Hasson has studied how specific neural patterns play out in our brains with stories. Hasson conducts experiments in which he measures brain activity with a functional MRI (fMRI) while listeners are told a personal story. The brain activity of the listener was similar to the storyteller. The similarities in brain activity is called neural coupling or mirroring. It shows that listeners will not only experience similar brain activity to the others in the group, but also to the speaker. The emotional regions of the listeners' brains are activated at the same time and in similar patterns to the speaker's brain. Not surprisingly, the study showed that the stronger the coherence between brain patterns, the deeper the understanding between the teller and the audience.

We think in story. It's hardwired in our brain. It's how our subconscious makes quick decisions and how we make sense of the world around us because the brain is seeking meaning from countless inputs and remembers them — not perfectly, but by stitching together memories, events, feelings, and ideas into an imperfect "story" for future reference. Our brain is actually *programmed* to process information through storytelling. These aren't literally stories as we experience them through a teller, but our minds are programmed to recognize patterns of information and assign them meaning. It's how we learn to associate facial features with a specific person, or music notes with a particular song. With reflexive automaticity, our subconscious brain looks for patterns from memory, from past experiences, from stories and uses them to make instantaneous decisions about current circumstances. Neuroscientist Antonio Damasio says, "The problem of how to make all this wisdom understandable, transmissible, persuasive, enforceable — in a word, of how to make it stick — was faced and a solution was found. Storytelling was the solution. Storytelling is something brains do, naturally and implicitly... It should be no surprise that it pervades the entire fabric of human societies and culture."

We listen intently to other people's stories. Anthropologically, others' stories provide survival lessons. If we could only use our own experiences, from a survival standpoint, we'd never make it. Stories share experiences, and shared experiences improve our survival. You didn't need to live through a flood. You didn't need to randomly determine the best weapon to kill a bear. You didn't need to risk eating the red berries or funny looking mushrooms. Shared stories have created a mental encyclopedia of lessons. We have hard-wired expectations for the stories told to us. It's not the lyrical prose that captures our attention; it's the story's ability to provide the kind of information we need for survival. Stories create mental rehearsals.

Some stories have staying power. They're recalled effortlessly as reminders, as signposts, as whispers of encouragement. Some stories can be powerful, timeless, boundaryless because they cut to the core of what it means to be human, tapping into deep hidden motives, and even neurologically coupling experiences between strangers. Your stories have value long after you tell them. They imprint and connect to the listener in ways unknown to you, but there is a very real biological basis for our attraction to story. When we tell stories, not only do we celebrate ordinary men and women with surpassing kindness, boundless bravery, relentless hope, unwavering character, steadfast leadership, fastidious fortitude, but we encode these traits to the listener. Our stories can be embedded in others' memory so there is an involuntary retrieval of it when it's needed, truly passing lessons and experiences on to others. Storytelling magically involves the mingling of the teller and listener that transcends time, sharing not just words and history, but emotions and experiences. Stories can deeply imprint your values and lessons so others can spontaneously recall them in their everyday lives.

A story can go to places where data can't — our hearts. Data might convey, but it doesn't inspire people to act, because data doesn't fire up the imagination and the soul. Credibility counts, but people need to feel things to elicit action. Unlike statistics, stories trigger emotions. The Significant Objects Project is a literary and anthropological experiment set out to determine if the value of an object — mostly worthless flea market items — can be affected by the story behind it. Invented stories are written about practically worthless items to see whether an imaginative story can enhance each object's value. For instance, there were monkey hand puppets said to have been used to teach children to speak; there were cat bowls said to have been used to feed felines who provided companionship through a difficult divorce. Dozens of insignificant objects — all with avowed fictional stories — sold for more than 1000% of their actual value because an imaginative story transformed rubbish to something treasured. Experiencing a story alters our neurochemical pathways. Studies also show that our brain is highly engaged with stories.   Facts and data only activate two parts of the brain, but brain imaging studies have shown that listening to stories can activate up to seven regions of the brain (more than math or music) — the motor cortex, sensory cortex and cerebellum, auditory center in Broca's area, language processing in Wernicke's area, olfactory cortex, auditory cortex, and visual cortex. We try to compel people with facts and figures, but the result isn't sticky. Stories are sticky.

Stories Imprint deep into our Memories
We don't think stories, we *feel* stories.

The human memory is biased. Our memories aren't an exact reflection of the things we've experienced. We don't remember with details, we remember with feelings. We don't think in words but in emotionally charged images.   Neuroscientists are finding that memories aren't stored with logic. The language of the brain is images, feelings, experiences.

Emotion signals to the brain that something is important — *pay attention!* Stories change brain chemistry by actuating neurotransmitters. Neurotransmitters are chemicals that neurons use to communicate with each other. They govern feelings and emotions; they are the language of the brain. The longer neutrons fire, the more that fire, the more intensely they fire, the more they are going to tag that memory. The right mix of neurotransmitters are elicited depending on the story. Where a thought goes, a chemical follows. If a story has a happy ending, it triggers the limbic system to release dopamine and we get a burst of optimism. If a story has elements of danger or suspense, then our hippocampus releases cortisol which sharpens attention and boosts strength and speed.

When we are trusted or shown kindness, our body produces the hormone oxytocin. Some call oxytocin the moral molecule or the love hormone. Oxytocin spurs us to help others, engenders hope, and prompts voluntary cooperation. When our brain synthesizes oxytocin, we are more generous, trustworthy, compassionate, caring, considerate, charitable. If I am treated well or connect with someone, then my brain will synthesize oxytocin and treat another person well in return.

Researchers have found that stories promote oxytocin synthesis in our brains. Oxytocin production motivates pro-social behaviors such as cooperation, generosity, trustworthiness, compassion, love and social connection to others. The amount produced by the brain can predict how much people are willing to help others. In research studies at Claremont University, Dr. Paul Zak found that oxytocin synthesis produced by the brain predicted how much people were willing to help others. So when we tell stories, we enlist the cooperation of others by empathetically creating a shared experience. We empathize with the storyteller so that we share a common emotion.

What does all of this mean for those who want to be legacy leaders? Credibility counts for a lot, but ultimately you must make an audience feel something to encode a memory, to get your story to stick.

Legacy leaders create signature stories.

Stories tap into universal human truths. Stories give our struggle meaning, because meaning is the vein that runs through great stories. It runs through your story. Think of an organization as a big conversation, an ongoing storytelling event.

How did we get here?

How did we get through that? That crisis, that tragedy, that misfortune?

What enabled our success?

How did we get stuck and then unstuck?

Legacy leaders are aware of the stories that need to be told. They look at the conditions in their teams and the circumstances they are facing, then they find the story that needs to be written.

They don't just anticipate the future, they shape it with a conscious choice to make an impact. With keen discernment and mindfulness, they see their present circumstances as fertile ground to build a signature story. These signature stories are powerful — for building confidence and capability, for building identity, for building character, for growing apprentices, for transforming teams and organizations. These signature stories have staying power because of their underlying significance to people and the organization, even the leader. Stories increase both our self-awareness and self-development. Your signature stories define who you are and who you want to become. Signature stories emerge from epic journeys.

Great stories have similar ingredients — universal longings that move us — love, adventure, danger, romance, heroism, sacrifice, good vs. evil, insurmountable odds, hope. Great stories follow a similar pattern — things were good, something awful happened, and now a great battle must be fought, a journey must be taken. Change has an identifiable pattern to it and it follows the structure of an epic adventure.

Leaders manage change. Characters are like travelers, leaving familiar territory and travelling through unknown lands to seek reward. Along the way, the hero is tested, faces challenges and is ultimately changed. People love these stories because they mirror the kind of struggles we encounter and hopefully overcome in our lives. Scientists have found that the brain is attracted to a specific kind of story — the epic journey.

The epic journey is one of the most powerful and dramatic forms a story can take. It's a journey of transformation marked by moments of defeat and moments of triumph. A character grows by overcoming something whether it be external or internal. Human struggle then eventual triumph. Without it, there is no meaning or perspective. Without it, there is no yearning for better. Without it, there is no desire to become someone better. The lives of your team, your organization, your apprentices and yes, your leadership is a series of epic journeys — heroic quests.

In 1863, a German novelist, Gustav Freytag used a pyramid to describe how narratives follow a common pattern or dramatic arc. There is a pivot – a turning point, a turn-around — what is called the dramatic arc. The dramatic arc is a structure with an overall shape of rising and falling tension or conflict. This rise and fall generates substantial emotion. This tension captures our attention and leaves us wanting to know more. Researchers have shown through MRI studies that sustained attention in stories is most often achieved through the dramatic arc. The dramatic arc is often used by screenwriters and novelists to underscore change in the character. The events of every great story are conduits to emphasize the human change, the personal growth.

Tension + Pivot + Resolution = Personal Growth

Great stories have a few other essentials. Great stories need relatable characters so listeners can empathize, "put themselves in their shoes," and mirror the story as it unfolds. Great stories need unexpectedness and curiosity. Great stories have something at stake, a gap between what is and what could be; this tension gives the story weight and attracts our brain's attention.

Using inspiration from acclaimed storyteller Nancy Duarte, a framework for organizing signature stories was created — Epic Journey Storycrafting. The framework can help make sense of experiences and events through the lens of moments. At these moments something hangs in the balance. There is a decision — a call to action — that must be addressed. It's at these moments where legacy stories have their center of gravity. It's at these moments when we experience something that grows us, teaches us, demands something from us, pulls us, pushes us and nudges us to move.

Preparing to Get Inspired by Your Epic Journey

You can start by identifying signature events. While your memory likely hinges on one moment, each significant event likely spans across multiple moments. For example, a decision to initiate a product recall or exit a market or product isn't isolated to the moment. Rather, that moment is built up to. There was the moment of inspiration to face the truth, the moment of tension when a choice needed to be made, and the moment when you leaped forward without knowing the consequences. There were likely many moments within the journey, smaller epiphanies that gave you courage or direction. Signature events have unlikely beginnings and endings; they are connected through golden threads of experiences.

Beginning

In every great story, there is a tension — a tension between what is and what could be, between the dream and the reality, between the starting point and the desired finishing point. The tension sparks our neurological-attention pathways and draws us in; the tension creates empathy; the tension puts the story in motion. The beginning unveils our shot at redemption.

Your myth of origin. *Once upon a time.* The formation of your principles and character. The conditions that nurtured, almost predisposed, your character, mindset, attitudes and behaviors. The starting point; the FROM state.

Moment of Rousing / Call to Dream: *But I dreamed...* When you dream of something better or when you realize that something must change.

Middle

The middle underscores the decision to break the tension, to change, to turnaround, to revolt, to transform. It is effectively a leap into the unknown with the hope of a bright future. But things aren't always as they seem. Under adversity, a struggle ensues — to give up or bravely face the climb. The external conditions are shaping, molding, forging something fledgling internally. The experiences are growing us, awaking something hidden in us, preparing us.

Moment of Decision / Facing the Leap. *Then finally one day...* The conditions of the past are in conflict with the pull of the future. The IS state vs. the COULD BE state. That unsettled feeling of being stuck, being at odds with your principles, the calling for something more or something to be done. Without safety nets, the character answers the call to adventure and takes a leap of faith. The hero chooses to leave the safety and security of the present for the hope of the unknown future.

Moment of Adversity / Facing the struggle. *Never had they faced something so...* This is the unexpected struggle, the fight, and it calls forth hidden courage, boldness, fortitude.

Moment of Desperation / Facing the Abyss. *When all seemed lost...* When darkness closes in, hardship is at its peak, the circumstances are pressing, the hero must rely on his strength and still hope.

Defining Moment. *But then...* The pivot and turning point for the hero; she must decide to turn away or face into the storm; he must decide to turn toward the giant or retreat.

Moment of Endurance / Facing the Reality of the Climb. While the thrill of victory euphorically carries characters temporarily, they inevitability get a little lost and a little lonely. The stark reality of trying circumstances and fleeting stamina brings them to their knees. There is a crossroads of exhaustion.

End

The end isn't simply a ceasing of the strenuous ordeals and trials, the quandaries and predicaments. The end is the triumph leading to self-discovery and growth. The original vision may or may not have been achieved. Almost certainly, the original plans didn't work as the hero had predicted. But the beauty of the ending has everything to do with what the hero found inside of himself or herself.

Moment of Discovery / Facing triumph. *Finally...* When desperation sets in, when all seems lost, personal growth happens through self-discovery. A new character is formed.

EPIC JOURNEY STORYCRAFTING

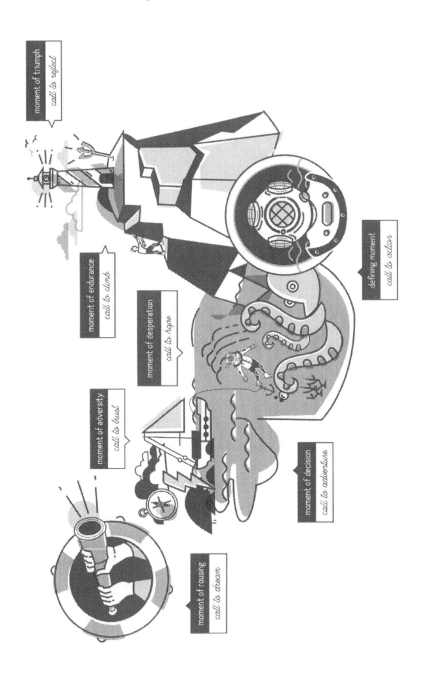

You have experienced numerous heroic quests throughout your life. They may not be neatly sequenced. They may be a jumbled hodgepodge of seemingly unrelated ups and downs. But they are uniquely your stories and there are lessons in them. There is a purpose in your stories. Tell us your stories. Authentically. Vulnerably. Don't shy away from the lessons, from the adversity. Adversity introduces us to ourselves. Those moments which we so desperately wanted to simply go-away at the time were the very moments that unearthed buried character traits, gifts and passions. Human struggle grows us.

When you look at your epic journeys, can't you see that you grew most when the circumstances demanded it from you? When you weren't ready. Hardship introduces us to inner transformation; it puts us on stage in gripping, heart-pounding, fist pumping scenes. There is tension and tragedy in your story, in every story. Let it mean something. Reveal the legacy lessons through your stories.

Legacy Story Starters

Be a story archeologist. Find a quiet, comfortable place with a cup of coffee or tea and read the words below. Pause at each and simply jot down what experience comes to mind. Don't feel like you need to write more than a few bullets or sentences. Some experiences you'll want to contemplate longer. Write down some details, think about the epic-journey moments in the framework on the previous page. Write down your emotions. Don't filter. Let the words come forth.

> Your values tested...when something was on the line
> Conviction
> Determination
> Boldness
> Perseverance
> A leap of faith
> Hope
> Resilience

Redemption

Dreaming of something new

Transformation

Desperation

Afraid

A turning point

A turnaround

Feeling stuck

Facing a giant

Look at the Epic Journey Storycrafting and find experiences in your life that fit with the *Moments* and *Calls to Action*. Think about how, in that experience, the moments and calls to action played out; how they summoned your character. How did you grow through the different stages? How did this experience mark you? What was different from one side of the moment to the other side; I was _____ but then I was _____. Find your signature stories embedded in this experience.

Looking back or looking ahead find events with gaps between *what is* and *what could be*.

Look for the *but...then* moments as the signals to your signature stories.

3 THE 7 ESSENTIAL STORIES OF EVERY LEADER

In our organizations and corporations, individual identities tend to get lost. Telling personal stories and team stories may be one of the few means of humanizing our work and communicating our wisdom and our hope to others.   Our tendency is to influence and communicate through decks and dictums, assuming that perfectly rational people will accept our perfectly rational ideas, pitches, decisions, and directives. But people don't want more information – more facts and figures. They've had enough information dumped on them. They want to hope in where you are taking them. They want to believe in their organization and in their team. They want a story that inspires them, that's meaningful, that makes a difference.

What stories are told around your board table? Around your conference rooms? Around your water cooler, coffee machines and break rooms? What tales are told across your desk to willing and unwilling listeners? What stories do you tell your clients, your customers, your suppliers? What stories do you tell your new employees? What stories speak volumes about your organization – your meager origins, your steadfast values, your enduring beliefs, your audacious vision, your setbacks and your comebacks? What signature stories are told about your team to attract future talent, to reinforce your culture and expectations?

Story is the language of the heart. Life — professionally and personally — unfolds like a beautiful story. Scene by scene. Chapter by chapter. Moment by moment. We often don't know what happens next. It doesn't show up or come to us in neatly organized bits or structured like an algebra problem. It is rich with comedy and drama, tragedy and adventure, hardship and adulation. It is steeped with interesting characters, twisted circumstances, and "you-can't-make-this-stuff-up" plots. We are often thrown into the middle of stories, only to put our own fingerprints on the next chapters.

Every leader has a story to tell. Every team, every organization, every mentee deserves a leader who can grow them through stories. During a leader's tenure, certain stories will almost inevitably be called upon because circumstances create the obligation for leaders to respond, to model, to calm, to face into, to prepare, to inspire, to teach, to lead. But there are other moments when it's not so obvious that a story should be told. It's in those moments that you may miss the opportunity to provide what the organization so desperately needs — a moral compass, the searing truth, optimism, a lesson from the past, a metaphor that reframes their perspective. A presentation just won't do when you are facing a crisis of confidence. A deck just won't do when you step into a new role.

Some leaders naively drown their audience in facts and figures in an effort to convince them to do something. If *knowing* were the sole precursor to *doing,* then decks packed with bullets and graphs, pie charts and pedagogic language would compel us to get up out of our chairs and start moving. It can happen, but it's rare. There is a long distance between knowing what to do and actually doing it. Participants can walk away from masterfully-prepared decks smarter, but not emboldened to achieve; informed, but not motivated to do; clear on the what, but unmoved on the why; aware of the company position, but without heartfelt hope.

Then there are those impending moments that need to be written. With keen instincts, legacy leaders see the potential in certain moments to be epic. They see their importance to apprentices, their team and organizations. They see the potential signature story in the moment — the turnaround, the comeback, the never-again story that must-be written. They even create the conditions for new stories to be written. They aren't just adept at finding the stories from their history, but they know when and how to create the stories that will be told in the future.

Your Essential Stories

You are both the curator of stories — an esteemed collector of great stories — and an architect of stories – a planner for the stories that want to be, need to be written in the future. The foundations of legacy — Apprenticing, Boldness, Connection and Culture — are nurtured, imprinted, and cultivated through stories. There are seven essential stories for legacy leaders. While a leader can't predict every occasion or orchestrate every set of circumstances, there are stories that every leader will need on their legacy journey. As a story curator you need to have a repertoire of essential stories that can be called upon at a moment's notice. Some may be your very own signature stories, they might be stories of someone else's defining moment or they might be legendary stories passed down with unmistakable significance. Stories are the stones for building legacy so you need to have plenty of them, and you need to know when and where to place them. As a legacy leader you need to be prepared with a story: not one that is perfectly delivered nor one just casually pulled out of your pocket, but instead one that is thoughtfully and carefully contemplated and chosen. You need to be a master builder that pulls out the right story stone that fits the occasion.

You can also use the essential stories to be attentive to moments ripe for future storytelling. Everyday moments or defining moments can take on more meaningful significance by asking, *what story do I want to tell?*

THE 7 ESSENTIAL STORIES OF THE LEGACY LEADER

The Story	Similar Stories	Imprints to Listener/Enables action to…
The Comeback Story	But…Then Story Goliath-Must-Fall Story	Imprints resilience, hope, courage to face adversity; gets a team over a hump or challenge. Finds meaning in an impossible challenge leading to self-discovery and transformation.
From…To Story	Stall Story Why-we-need-to-change story	Depicts why the status quo is dangerous, why we are changing and what will happen if we don't change. Faces the brutal facts, unlearns the past, and creates a future. Helps them get "unstuck" on their own; can help them lead small or sizable revolutions
Defining-Moment Story	At-the-Crossroads Story Leap-and-Climb Story	Imprints wisdom, cautionary lessons by using hindsight to see with foresight; teaches personal and professional character lessons for thoughtful decision-making; shares knowledge by focusing on mistakes made or victories won
Let me tell you what ___ looks like Story	What-We-Have-Learned Story Label Story Gratitude Story	Puts values and principles in action; sets high expectations so that good is the enemy of great; celebrates a character trait in someone; expresses deep gratitude; fosters identity creation in teams and mentees to unlock potential and allow them to see themselves differently. Transmits values in action
If-not-you-then-who Story	It's-Your-Turn Story Because-Only-You-Can Story	Insists on action without being ready; imprints perseverance and grittiness to stay the path. Encourages others to build something worth contributing to; questions self-imposed limits; fosters deep personal/team accountability.
Who-am-I / Who-We-Are Story	Myth-of-Origin Story	Communicates who you are by beautifully revealing your vulnerability and humanness; Imparts connection and identity to the heart of people and roots of an organization; reveals who you are as a person or organization — your journey, character and valuable lessons; powerful communication tool for stakeholders, employees, partners, prospects
What if…Vision Story	Undiscovered-Country Story The-Great-Unfinished-Work Story	Imprints hope and expectations of the future; demonstrates how to see things differently to improve the world around us; shows how to turn vision into reality; imagines vivid images of what the future may hold so others imagine it with you; allows listeners to dream, suspend judgement, and move from can't to can do. Leads people into the future you want to create without excessive detail

A note on story content for your essential stories. It's fine to use other people's stories or metaphors as examples to get your point across, to illustrate a circumstance that may not have happened to you but could, to arouse the audience with a dramatic arc, to help them to relate. Sometimes, others' stories are deeply personal to you and are therefore authentically part of your story. You'll see examples where someone else's story can assist in your message.

Your Signature Stories about you and your team

Your signature stories are your personal assets with enduring relevance. Your signature stories carry through the veins of your organization, your values, your meaning, your why. They are a key tool to transfer wisdom, to illuminate a compelling vision, to carry values forward, to motivate change, to humanize you. Just like your handwritten signature, your signature stories are unique to you and your organization. Written in your voice, your tone, your colloquialisms, they mean something to you because they come from the depths of your struggle, your victories, your values, your vision. They mean something to your people because someone else's story becomes their story in the tribe of your organization. Your stories are both deeply personal and easily accessible by others, but they need exposure — they need a light shined on them. They need to be known, seen, heard, and shared.

Your need some bravery to tell your signature stories. Signature stories about yourself are radically transparent. They don't conceal mistakes, not-so-proud moments or errors, but their openness builds deep and enduring trust. This can be scary because we worry that authentically disclosing our foibles and flaws will cause others to think less of us. Quite the counter is true. As one worker said, "The true test of a great leader is their willingness to admit that they aren't perfect. That makes them real, relatable, and worthy of my candidness."

Your *Who-Am-I* stories allow people to connect with you not only as a leader, but also as a person. These stories can accelerate months, maybe years, of time getting to know you by illuminating thin slices of your character, your non-negotiables, your expectations, and your principles in very real and human ways. People need to decide about you for themselves — not through accolades from your bio or impressive results listed on your CV, but with a story. These stories can marginalize hearsay and rumors, dispel facades and falsehoods, and bring the real you, in your words, from the depths of your reality. Your *Who-Am-I* stories can diffuse the preconceived notions and perceptions we carry of larger-than-life, power-hungry leaders by exposing your realness. You need to win the hearts of your teammates; you need to gain their trust. This story says you are human, that you are part of "us." Being part of "us" invites you into their "tribe."

Your people may not understand where you are going, but they have to believe in you. They may not understand the changes you are recommending, but they need to trust you. People may make false impressions, snap judgements, stereotypes, wrong assumptions until they walk a while in your shoes. Let your stories reveal the real you, the vulnerable you, the person behind the title.

Bob Knowling, former CEO of US West, often tells the story of a watershed moment for him and his family. As a young boy, he was with his mother, a single mom raising thirteen kids, at the grocery store one day when she tried to use food stamps to buy peanut butter. The clerk spoke disrespectfully: "If you didn't have so many kids, you wouldn't need to worry about peanut butter."

At that moment, Knowling remembers, his mother made a decision. Outside the store she took his hand and told him, "I am off welfare forever." After that, she took a string of different jobs, often working day and night, but she kept her resolve, and the family stayed off welfare. According to Knowling, the courage and persistence he saw in her has stayed with him since. Asked what drives him, Knowling points to a couple of things: "The rough road of my childhood...all of that is the reservoir of strength that I draw from," he says. "My mom is my hero... I witnessed the transformation of my mom, and my own began as well. And I always keep in mind that at the end of the day, failure isn't an option."

Preparing your *Who-Am-I* Stories

Mapping Your Life Journey. Map your journey of life's triumphs and defeats. Our experiences teach us things and crystalize our teachable points of view.

Make a sideways "T" on a piece of length-wise paper. The "y" axis denotes your emotional state — either positive or negative, and the "x" axis is time. Plot life events — personal and professional experiences and signature moments — as marks in time (on the x axis) and emotion (on the y axis). Think about your early years in school, in your family, in your profession. Think about your defining moments, trying experiences, bold moves, mistakes, misfortunes, tragic circumstances, watershed moments, proud moments. Look for the salient stories. Don't worry if you think nobody will find them interesting. Look for those stories that say something about you — who you are, where you come from, why you are who you are, why you hold fast to certain truths, principles, values and beliefs. This same exercise can be done for teams or organizations.

Reflect on the lessons at some of the markers in your life. What did you learn? What experiences helped define you? How did these milestones and defining moments shape you as a leader? How did certain experiences grow your character or elicit new character traits? Identify the labels you carried with you.

What were particularly challenging events or periods? What did you learn from them? What did you learn about yourself?

Think about the key players in your life — journey companions, your cheering section, master builders. What lessons did you learn from your heroes, master builders, influencers?

When you string them together or look to connect the dots, how would you describe what you stand for, what is important to you, what you are passionate about, what principle(s) you hold tightly? Write a *Who-I-Am* story from this.

Your why story. Your why story hands down, may be one of the most important and powerful stories you have. It gets to the heart of your intention, your motivation, your passion. Why do you work? Why do you do the work that you do?

Reflected Best Self. Based on the empirical research from University of Michigan's Center for Positive Organizations, the Reflected Best Self (RBS) Exercise uses stories collected from people in all contexts of life to help them see who they are and how they contributed when they were at their best. By using RBS, we can elucidate our extraordinary moments, those moments when we felt that we demonstrated our best self, which others have affirmed.

Ask fifteen people from former bosses to work colleagues, from coaches and teammates to friends and family members, from community volunteers to current and former apprentices to write a story about a time when you made an important contribution either through a person, a project, a character trait, or some other way. Read these stories and look for patterns of who you are at your best. What are your strengths or "super-powers"? What hidden or unnoticed traits and skills surprised you?

Preparing for new situations. In any new assignment, team or organization, even new customer conversations, you need to be prepared to answer the question "Where do you come from?" "From" has lots of meaning — your early job experiences, your formative experiences, your place of origin. Where you come from speaks volumes about you and why you have your beliefs and values. While it may not be your formal introduction or a first impression, it has a profound priming effect. Think about answering the question, "Where do you come from," using three different stories with three different meanings of the word "from."

Massive mistakes. Real people make mistakes. In a world of hyperbole and hubris, of an escalating race to amass social-media likes, it's easy to dismiss mess-ups or deflect them as someone else's fault. But people can sniff out falsehoods. The true test of vulnerability for legacy leaders is a willingness to share the rawness of your mistakes so apprentices don't repeat them. The real test of mistakes is what you make from them. Your mistakes could help foster your team's growth. What stories would reveal a colossal mistake, a vulnerability, a weakness so that others can feel your authenticity and humanness? What did you learn from it?

The Seven Basic Plots. Christopher Booker worked on *The Seven Basic Plots: Why We Tell Stories* for thirty-four years before publishing in 2004. The book identifies seven basic plots across the vast universe of stories from Hollywood to bedtime stories to Aesop's fables. Booker says, "How ever many characters may appear in a story, its real concern is just with one: its hero or heroine. It is (s)he with whose fate we identify, as we see him or her gradually developing towards a state of self-realization which marks the end of the story. Ultimately it is in relation to this central figure that all other characters in the story take on their significance." According to Booker, the following are the seven fundamental plots:

Overcoming the Monster. The character sets out to defeat a villain who threatens the character or what's important to the character (e.g., family, homeland). Examples: James Bond stories, *Star Wars*, *The Hunger Games*.

Rags to Riches. The poor character acquires things such as power, wealth, or a mate, before losing it all and then gaining it all back while growing as a person. Examples: *Aladdin*, *Cinderella*, *David Copperfield*, *Jane Eyre*.

The Quest. The character and some companions set out to acquire an important object or get to a location to realize a dream, facing many obstacles and conflicts that grow them as a person. Examples: *The Lord of the Rings*, *Harry Potter*, *Raiders of the Lost Ark*, *Lara Croft*.

Voyage and Return. The character leaves his/her homeland, and, after overcoming conflicts, returns with experience. Examples: *Goldilocks*, *The Odyssey*, *The Hobbit*, *Apollo 13*, *The Chronicles of Narnia*, *The Wizard of Oz*.

Comedy. A light and humorous character overcomes

adverse circumstances to triumph in a happy ending. Examples: *Mr. Bean, Four Weddings and a Funeral, A Midsummer Night's Dream, Bridget Jones' Diary.*

Tragedy. The character is a hero with a major flaw or a great mistake which begins to unravel their life in unfortunate ways. Examples: *Macbeth, Romeo and Juliet, Hamlet, Breaking Bad*

Rebirth. The character grows in wisdom and maturity over the course of the story, making him or her a better person. Examples: *A Christmas Carol, Beauty and the Beast, How the Grinch Stole Christmas.*

Think about experiences in your life that fit in each of these plots. Don't take the story plots literally, but consider them as metaphors in your life. Look at your Life Journey Map and identify the seven basic plots in your experiences. Use the plots to write some story starters.

Examples of *Who-I-Am Stories*:

Share

There are few days in the year more exciting for me then when we give out annual bonuses. Sure, the extra cash is great. But for me, well, it's personal. I remember starting my first job out of college. I worked like crazy — nights, weekends — trying to develop a new product. And we did. Something patentable and pretty remarkable. I overheard my manager bragging one day about how big his bonus was going to be that year — bigger than the salary of some people in his department —and what toys and vacations he was going to spend his enormous bonus on. I was the lowest paid person in the department. A range of emotions swelled up inside me...but mostly anger. Anger over his arrogance. Anger over the injustice of all of us contributing, but only one of us getting the reward. Sure, I was a little naïve fresh out of college. But I made a promise that day that I've kept for years: when I get a bonus, I will share it with everyone on my team who doesn't get a bonus. Sure enough, about five years later I was promoted to a team leader. I received my first bonus and I shared it with everyone on my team — I wrote them each a personal check. I received postcards from vacation destinations, pictures of home renovations, and names of children with more in their college fund savings. In disbelief someone thought there must be strings attached — *Why would you share your money with us?* "Because *we* delivered the results and *we* will share in the reward...*I* didn't do it alone."

Why I'm so passionate about Work-Family Balance

University of Michigan professor Jeff DeGraff has been studying work-family balance issues for decades. He said something that stuck with me, "The deeper issue is that we are addicted to work. This is not a minor issue. In our culture, work has become fundamental to our identity. It is a socially sanctioned addiction." At that time, I was a workaholic.

I wish I could say that my realization was painless, but it wasn't. I had a pregnant wife and young toddler at home. I was putting in more than sixty-hour weeks. I was trapped in a mindset that my self-worth was a reflection of my success at work. So I buried myself in work. I prioritized it over my family. I was selfish and insecure. I'd never say it like that. I'd say, "I am working hard to provide for my family." But it was a cover-up to a deep-seated, skewed belief that if I didn't succeed at work, then I was a failure. So for nearly twenty years, I've come home for dinner every night and rarely worked at night or on weekends. But you might find me on occasion secretly going into work at four a.m. to ensure I'm home for dinner so my kids know that work doesn't compete with them.

Culture will never tell you to work less. I probably won't either. Trust me, the work never ends. Yes, you contribute here and your work is seriously important, but you are never replaceable at home. You may never get applause or accolades, pats-on-the-back or kudos at home like you do at work, but your work there is preeminently important. You may never be truly missed at work, but you'll always be missed at home. Work-family balance — it's personal to me. I want you know why I am so passionate about it. I've felt the guilt, the tightrope walking, the tug-o-war between responsibilities at home and those at work. When you see me leave at five p.m. every day, I want you to know why. When I don't respond to emails at night or weekends, I want you to know why. I want you to know where I stand.

Overcoming Hidden Bias

My first leadership lesson came from a high school drop-out. I had been assigned to a high priority project as a lead scientist. We were developing flushable/biodegradable products to reduce the environmental impact of our disposable products. To evaluate the "flushability" of certain products, I needed to test dozens of materials and product designs. So I built a toilet stand with several different kinds of toilets, a simulated sewer system and began countless flushing experiments. (Yeap, I started my illustrious career flushing toilets). I asked for a technician to assist me in literally hundreds of these flushing experiments every day.

Tracy came with a reputation as a lazy technician and a recovering alcoholic. Several people would roll their eyes when I mentioned her name. "She can't think for herself," I was told. So I treated Tracy based on what I'd learned from the perceptions of others. I never really tried to get to know her. I'd just ask her to "just give me the data."

She would often make observations in the margins of data sheets she gave me every day, but I never paid attention to them. I'd politely hear her, but never really listen; I just wanted the data.

After a few months of working with Tracy, I grew to respect her unbelievable work ethic. She never complained about repeating the same mindless task — flushing and recording — over and over all day. She enjoyed what she did and saw it as interesting.

121

One day I actually listened to one of Tracy's observations. She revealed an incredible insight that became the foundation for the rapid development of the project. "I have been telling you this for a while," she politely reminded me as thanked her. I was so embarrassed. I had dismissed her contribution — her ideas and insights and analysis — for months.

Her fingerprints are on millions of products sold across the globe and a patent. Tracy was promoted — her first in decades — based on her keen observations and hard work. She was so proud to tell her husband, kids, and grandkids! Tracy had demonstrated potential for years, but no one had ever given her a chance and for months neither did I.

Many years after I left that team, I received an invitation 750 miles away for Tracy's retirement party. The note inside made me cry. Tracy thanked me for giving her an opportunity to prove her potential — to herself, her family, and her company. She was retiring with esteemed self-satisfaction.

That experience changed me. I never let others' perceptions keep me from seeing someone for who they really are. Now I give everyone a chance; then I give them a second chance just like Tracy gave me a second chance to be a better manager. I watch for the greatness in everyone. That greatness exists, but you need to look for it. Maybe, just maybe, I hope you'll have the incredible privilege of helping someone shower the world with their hidden potential. And in the process, you'll be changed too.

In his book, *The Brilliance of Failure,* Chris Brickman shares an email he sent to his team when he was president at a major company. His letter was sent to illuminate his own imperfections so his colleagues could understand him better and could give him feedback if they observed some of his behaviors. Here's a snapshot of what was in the email (for which he received, to his surprise, very positive feedback):

Perfection is a myth. We can pursue it, aspire to it, and desire it, but we will never achieve it. Despite this fact, we are often driven by the myth of perfection, and we agonize over failures, mistakes and shortcomings. I have witnessed very capable leaders worry that their issues or development areas would be perceived as serious weaknesses that might undermine their career paths.

As a result, they sometimes went to great lengths to hide or cover them up, which was futile because we all saw them, and the cover-up just looked silly (or worse — dishonesty). It is ironic that their attempts to be perfect actually diminished their impact as leaders.

I know that I felt this way as a young leader, and it drove some terrible leadership behavior on my part. I wanted so badly to show that I could be the perfect leader that I sometimes failed to be straightforward, direct, and honest with my team. As a result, it undermined their trust in me. I still agonize over results and performance. I got this from my mom, who was incredibly demanding of herself and her kids. My upbringing makes me prone to launching too many ideas and initiatives because I so desperately want to improve and win. I have to work at staying focused on the big ideas and ask others to challenge me if I am distracting the team. I fight this every single day I come to work...

Your *Who-We-Are* stories help organizations and teams embrace shared identity and what they are capable of becoming. They consist of collective experiences that can express the heart of a team or organization with searing simplicity. These grand stories can reveal hidden values and principles as well as illuminate unknown sacrifices and bold decisions that can propel confidence and inspire change. By imprinting people with a common heritage, they live up to the standards and examples of their shared identity.

People don't buy into your organization, they buy into the difference you make. Your company needs to communicate a great backstory about why your organization exists and why your idiosyncrasies — your archaic ways of doing things, your old-fashioned values — are fundamental, not fleeting. Every great company has a quest that addresses a human need. Our organizational quests can easily get lost in complexity or crisis. *Who-We-Are* stories can reawaken and revitalize them.

According to Dr. Robert Cialdini, professor of Psychology at Arizona State University, creating a sense of identity inside the boundary of "we" is powerful. Identity through "we" stories creates belonging, affiliation, connectedness, and goodwill. "We" goals and beliefs build trust. By pointing to collective experiences, teams cooperate more, see more commonalities, and overlook differences. Pointing to traditions pulls people to belong, to be a socially connected part of something bigger than themselves.

Employees and customers alike must understand why your company exists. People can choose to work for almost anyone, and customers can choose to buy from almost anyone. The secret lies in the stories we tell. The *Who-we-Are* stories we tell over dinner to a customer can move your partnership from transactional to relational. The little stories we tell around the office can build pride and loyalty among teams. When new recruits ask about what it's like to work for your company in a job interview, your *Who-we-Are* stories can be talent magnets. Storytelling, as a form of organizational folklore, has been found to build organizational culture, shape team identity, and stabilize amid challenging circumstances.

Examples of *Who-We-Are* Stories:

Dignity is Who We Are

I was a newly appointed leader of a small business unit–very green, little experience and only a few years out of MBA school. Pete, my counterpart who ran the other half of the business, was a sharp, middle-aged retired Air Force captain. In fact, his persona at work was that of a "commander." He was tough, stubborn, proud, a little abrasive and he certainly wasn't a very collaborative colleague. He dismissed many of my ideas as "academic" and "would never work in the real world." He was intensely competitive keeping scorecards on customer wins, financial metrics and team output. Our relationship started strained but I learned a lot from him.

A few years into my role, Pete had stroke. I took over his responsibilities for months while he rehabilitated. When he came back to work, it was clear he wasn't a hundred percent recovered. He was quite fatigued after a few hours. Often, he knew what he wanted to say, but he just couldn't get the words out of his mouth. His thinking was cloudy and repetitive. But the respect, patience and effort that our team provided him astounded me. Despite falling behind in our financial objectives, we pulled together and rallied around Pete with incredible focus to ensure he delivered his yearly results. He leaned on me and I worked liked crazy not to let him down.

I'll never forget the annual financial review with our CEO and CFO. Pete struggled presenting with salience and clarity. With choppy sentences he proudly reviewed his outstanding results...with the confidence of a commander. Our boss and executives patiently allowed him to review his material despite repeating items several times. They honored someone who had dedicated many years to our company, not by pandering to his illness nor being dismissive because of his inadequacies, nor impatiently waiting to get the answers they were seeking, but by dignifying his dedication. This is the company you work for. We have each other's backs. We rally together. We accomplish our goals and deliver our results but never at the expense of people.

We are Cancer-Free

When my doctor told me I had cancer, I fell to the floor. I was twenty-eight! I run marathons! I was away from my family in Colombia. I thought I had no one and feared facing cancer alone. But you [the employees of my company] brought me food, took me to my treatments when I was exhausted, invited me to stay in your homes. You made sure I never faced my greatest fear — facing cancer alone.

All I wanted to do was run. At first I was running away. But then you helped me run toward a brighter future. When I ran my marathon with cancer, your cheerful signs pulled me across to the finish line. I am not cancer-free, WE are cancer-free. Since then, I've poured my heart into this business because you poured your heart into my life.

Starting Over

On April 3, 2016, I prepared for a business trip to Dallas. As usual, I hugged and kissed my husband good bye, drove to the airport, boarded the plane. When the plane landed, I removed my phone from airplane mode and scanned texts. The first text was normal for a Sunday night. A group text between my two daughters and a close friend while watching *The Walking Dead*. 'Hey what the h_ll, they killed Glen." Suddenly the text messages turned to panic. "Mom you have to come home, Dad is having a stroke!"

Instantaneously life as we knew it no longer existed. It felt as though a tornado hit our house and took Greg, an amazing husband, father, friend. He was gone and I wasn't the same person.

Nine months later, disoriented, scared, scarred, hurting, aching, bitter and still in shock, I woke up in Sydney at 3:00 a.m. and realized I had to make a choice, I had to make a change. One year after my husband's death I left a thirty-year career as an executive in corporate America and joined two partners to create a company to make a difference in the world — to promote the best places on earth to work, shop, play and invest. We teach and mentor other leaders with the belief that in business, how you achieve is just as important as what you're striving for. If you want to partner with us, it's important you know where I come from.

Similar Stories: Myth-of-Origin

Your *Myth-of-Origin Story* gets to the roots of an organization, its beginning. Every myth of origin is a tale of creation, how organizations and leaders came into existence. A company's founding story can fill employees' hearts with motivation and inspire a deep connection to the purpose and brand. The company's myth of origin story makes employees feel anchored to what the company stands for, uniting people behind an enduring symbol of corporate identity. The myth of origin story creates a symbolic narrative as a collective, confederate metaphor. Research by HealthStream, Towers Watson, and the O.C. Tanner Institute reveals that, "Pride in the Corporate Symbol is one of the three components of driving employee engagement."

A great origin story is the epicenter of organizational identity. Nail it, and the story will be told and retold countless times, imprinting your values and identity to scores of employees, customers, and suppliers. Irresistible and sticky origin stories focus on a specific moment at the inception of the business. It could be when you first envisioned your product or service. It may be when a nagging problem fired you up to act, and then you persistently solved it. Centering on a moment alleviates the burden of trying to chronologically detail the unfolding series of events with unnecessary details.

We are who we are today because of what those before us told us, modeled for us, instilled in us, prepared us to carry on. How much do we really know about leaders, teams, organizations who rose from nothing to where they are today? Those who imprinted their stalwart values into the fabric of people so that customers experience those timeless values generations later? Founders who fearlessly outmaneuvered outsized competitors? Entrepreneurs who boldly innovated at the edge through ingenuity and sacrifice. Not through the pages of history textbooks nor corporate memos or social media feeds will we find their indelible mark, but through the stories you tell. Storytelling can be the golden threads that weave us together – generations of employees.

In a world where it's easy to seeing fixing broken things — broken strategies, misplaced priorities, forfeited market share — as an opportunity for starting over, maybe even distancing from the past, Hewlett-Packard is an interesting case. H-P recognized it had lost sight of its myth of origin. Meg Whitman, quoted in *Harvard Business Review*, writes of the company's turnaround based on getting re-connected to its founding principles.

"I said, 'What are the core values of this company? Let's identify what it does really well and do more of that as the anchor for the turnaround. Then let's make a to-do list of the things to be fixed.' So we went back to the core founding principles, and the company responded. It's very hard to kill founder-DNA, and that's a good thing for H-P. Dave Packard and Bill Hewlett have been away from the company for many years. There have been many acquisitions, many changes. But the core values still show through: the ability to do incredible innovation; a passion for customer support and service; a desire to give back to the community. Dave and Bill were social responsibility leaders and environmentalists before those were even terms. We may have fallen on

some hard times, but we're going to double down on those values."

For many of us, the original quest, the original vision, and the foundational dream have gone into hibernation. Processes, bureaucracy and the withering away of values can bury the founder's intent. There was a human need at the origin — an inspiration, an injustice, an important problem to solve. Companies with clear, motivating quests, a compelling mission that transcends profitability, create almost incalculable loyalty. Think of Tom's of Maine, Zappo's, L.L. Bean, Wegman's, Patagonia.

Some examples of myth-of-origin stories:

IKEA: Everyone who works at IKEA knows where its founder, Ingvar Kamprad, grew-up. Smaland is a region of Sweden that was traditionally a poor agricultural community with stony soil. Smaland farmers had to make a little go a long way: they cleared the rocky land to farm and used the rocks they cleared from the fields to make walls that divided their land. Smaland is where IKEA was founded. The stone walls of Smaland are such an important symbol to IKEA that many stores around the world have a picture somewhere in the building of a stone wall. It means nothing to the consumer, but it means everything to IKEA. It represents making a little go a long way. It means making affordable things that also work and last for "the many" — ordinary people whose lives are constrained, every day people who have big dreams for their homes but small resources.

Make-a-Wish: In the spring of 1980, a seven-year old boy, Chris Greicius, was dying of cancer when he asked his mom if he could be a police officer for a day to catch bad guys. The Arizona Department of Public Safety (DPS) approved the endeavor. Officer Frank Shankwitz drove his motorcycle and Officer Jim Eaves drove his patrol car to a helicopter transporting Chris from the hospital to the police headquarters. Chris received a police officer hat, an old officer badge and became Arizona's first and only honorary DPS officer. The next day he was given a police uniform made overnight by a local uniform shop, and motorcycle officer's wings after Chris used his battery-powered motorcycle to maneuver through cones in a mock-competence test. Chris died a few days later and he was given the ceremony of a fellow fallen officer. Frank along with fellow working-class DPS officers, friends and family were so moved by the experience with Chris that they started a wish-making foundation. The first donation was fifteen dollars given to Shankwitz by a grocery store manager. In the spring of 1981, the group had raised over two thousand dollars — enough to grant its first wish to Frank "Bopsy" Salazar who had leukemia just like Chris. He was granted all of his three wishes: to be a fireman, go to Disneyland and ride a hot air balloon.

Intel Inside: In the late 1980s with little interest from OEMs and end users to upgrade to Intel's flagship 386 processor from the 286 and with the 486 well under development, Intel faced a clogged pipeline for its microprocessors. Dennis Carter, an engineer turned technical assistant to the chief executive Andy Grove, illuminated a keen insight — Intel had been marketing exclusively to design engineers at PC companies, but they weren't making the buying decisions anymore, the marketing team was. They needed to reach them and PC buyers directly to sway them to choose the 386. A small task group came up with what became known as the graffiti campaign: ads showing a 286 logo crossed out in red spray paint, with copy explaining why the 386 was better. People came into stores asking for "the 386" as if it was the computer. This was the birth of consumer marketing in semiconductors. Carter borrowed from the consumer-goods industry's cooperative marketing model, putting three percent of its revenue from microprocessor sales into a fund that PC manufacturers could tap to pay for "co-op" advertising. In 2001 alone, approximately 150 million *Intel Inside* stickers were printed and more than $1.5 billion in *Intel Inside* brand communication was generated, making Intel the sixth most valuable brand in the world alongside Disney and Coke.

TRX: In 1997, Navy SEAL Randy Hetrick was deployed in Southeast Asia, where he was stationed in a remote warehouse for weeks with no way to exercise. He needed something to stay fit, so he grabbed an old jujitsu belt that he accidentally stuffed in his bag, threw it over a door, and started doing pull-ups. Today, athletes are using their own body weight with TRX exercise straps dangling from the ceiling in more than 25,000 gyms across the country and nearly all professional sports teams in the U.S. use them.

Clif Bar: Gary Erickson had been on a one hundred seventy-five mile biking adventure. After he ate five of the six energy bars he packed that day, he realized he just couldn't eat another unappetizing, hard-to-chew bar. He took his idea — making a wholesome bar to sustain energy without any butter, sugar or oil — to the best baker he knew, his mom. After six months of taste testing with friends and family and tossing out dozens of not-good-enough bars, Gary landed on a winning formula and launched CLIF Bar in honor of his father, Clifford, the man who introduced him to wilderness adventures and encouraged him to follow his passion in life. When Clif celebrates taking risks as a value — they call it taking the white roads (unmarked on maps) not the red roads (well-marked on maps) — you know where it's coming from.

Dyson: In 1979, James Dyson had a radical idea for a new vacuum cleaner — one that didn't use bags. The vacuum cleaner manufacturers shunned his designs. He built one prototype at a time, making one minor change at a time so he methodically knew what difference that one change made. Dyson built 5,127 prototypes before he got it right. When Dyson expresses one of its core values as "Solving problems that others ignore with new thinking," you know where it's coming from.

The myth of origin is almost taken for granted in many organizations, but it is a lighthouse. When an organization gets lost, you can always come back to the origin story: it anchors us, it reminds us of the humble beginnings, it reminds us to dream and persist. People are more motivated by an organization's transcendent purpose then their transactional or financial purpose. One of the foundations for trust is to feel knotted to the organization and where it came from. Like any relationship, when we know where someone (or some organization) comes from, we feel connected and united.

Example of *Myth-of-Origin* Story:

Our reputation is our advantage

You are part of the fabric of this family company started by my dad. You need to know who we are and where our values came from. To do that we need to go back to the beginning. My dad used to say that the best things in life are on the other side of hard work and a little bit of fear. Before "customer-centricity" became vogue, my dad ran this business putting the customer at the center of everything we did. When a customer hit hard times, he would extend credit when no one else would. Not when it was easy for us, but precisely when it was hard for us too. He'd say, "that's when you test your principles — not when it's easy, but when it's inconvenient. Deals, dollars and plans come and go, but people will never forget how you treat them."

I'll never forget one particularly difficult year for our industry. We really fell on hard times. Our customers were hit particularly hard. Some owed us a lot of money. We didn't have enough money for new shoes. My dad threw duct tape on the bottom of my tattered shoes and told me, "If Jimmy struggles to put food on the table for his kids — we can struggle too."

Customers would come for barbeques in our backyard, even Thanksgiving dinner occasionally. Like family, I'd hear my dad argue with his guests. I wondered why we would invite these people to our home. But at the end of the evening he'd give them a firm handshake. "We need to win together," he'd say. "If I win and you lose, then I don't really win in the end at all."

We have thrived when those around us have withered away, imploded, or been battered by our changing industry. Sure, it might seem like the way we do things is old school, out of sync or even outdated, but this is who we are, and these principles and values you see as you walk into the building every day I believe are timeless and are as true today as they were decades ago. Sure, we need to change: our systems need upgrading, our processes need improvement, we need to digitize more. But we won't ever change the fabric of who we are. When you walk into an industry trade show, you better believe our reputation — respect — precedes us. Not because our technology is particularly brilliant or our solutions out-of-this-world novel, but because when you buy from us, you get 'us' — all of us — with every transaction. And I can tell you it's worth a lot.

Preparing your Who-We-Are and Myth-of-Origin Stories

Reading the Tree Rings. If you think about an organization or a team like the growth of a tree, you can uncover some interesting things. The cross sectional cut of a tree manifests its history through the growth chart of its rings. Each spring and summer, the tree adds new layers of wood to its trunk. The wood formed in spring grows fast and is lighter because it consists of large cells. In summer, growth is slower, the wood has smaller cells, and is dark. When a tree is cut, the layers of growth appear as alternating rings of light and dark wood. If you count the dark rings, you can count the age of the tree. Let's create a metaphorical tree ring for your team or organization.

Narrow rings that go on for several years suggest a drought. Few things can stunt growth like lack of water. When has your team or organization been thirsty or experienced a drought?

Narrow rings can also indicate insect infestation. When has your team or organization been invaded, in a fight of its life?

A tree that's happy is getting lots of sunshine and rain; it will show rings that are relatively broad. When has your team or organization truly thrived?

Scarring can show the presence of forest fires. When has your team or organization felt the heat of a forest fire?

Rings wider on one side vs. the other indicate excessive winds or that something that was growing was pushed against the tree. This *reaction wood* helps support the side that was leaning. When has something pushed hard against your team or culture such that caused you to change direction, transition, or compensate for external forces?

Becoming a Corporate Archeologist. Become the person in your company who knows more about the history than anyone else. Project it in stories. Interview founders or people who have been with your company or brand for a long time. Find those stories that were signature for them — defining moments, tough decisions, crossroad choices. Write about the origins — perhaps the beginning, or the dream, the leap of faith, the trying early days and years of sacrifices.

What stories about your founders, your leaders and your team members need to be told because their relevance has timeless significance? What story lessons have been passed down the years like parables? You may not have the story perfect, but write what you know and have other people shape it.

Who are the legends in your company — people who deeply imprinted something into the code of the company? What are their stories that have imprinted the organization?

Identify the values and principles that your organization holds so sacred. Where did they come from? What holds your organization together? What is the glue in its values? Fill in the blank. A _____(company name employee) always _____ [or never _____]. Where did this come from?

Stories that inspire us to action

Your *Comeback Stories* imprint resilience. They symbolize courage and determination amid adversity; they make us stand up and cheer; they move us, motivate us, embolden us. We've all been lost, disoriented, wandering, wondering if we'd make it back. That's why comeback stories are so powerful because they are so relatable. We've all wanted a shot at redemption, a chance to prove ourselves, an opportunity to proven them wrong, a turn at seeing what we are made of. Everyone loves a comeback story because we are wired for hope, and comeback stories at their core embody hope.

At the heart of every comeback story is a bold choice. A bold choice to move forward or turn and walk away. A bold choice to lean in or retreat. A bold choice to accept the painful consequences or give up. A bold choice to venture into an unknown place or play it safe. All of us will face the crossroads of a choice. If you want your audience to get moving again when everything seems to have halted in the face of an uncertain future, then you need to tell them a story about how tragic events don't define you, but your attitude and behaviors do. If you want your audience to pick themselves up off the ground when they are devastated, then you need to tell them a story of redemption after falling; you need them to unleash the power of resilience inside them. If you want your team to keep trying when everything in them says stop, when their tanks are empty, then you need to tell them a story about the time when against-all-odds, persistence and determination pulled you through the most unlikely of circumstances. Your Comeback Stories give them the courage. Your Comeback Stories fuel their hope.

Hollywood has mastered the comeback story. Some of our favorite movies are comeback stories – *Rocky, Star Wars, Schindler's List, Milk, The Martian, Hoosiers, Iron Man, Napoleon Dynamite, Toy Story, The Matrix, Shawshank Redemption, Wonder, Rudy* and countless others. Comeback stories rouse emotions. We stand up and cheer, we cover our eyes, we smile, we tear. There's something in all of us that loves the comeback story because we are anthropologically motivated for personal growth. Not in the academic sense per se, but in the human sense — to be challenged and come up stronger. It's an innate human need built into our DNA for survival. We see ourselves — the best and worst of us — in the shoes of characters in comeback stories.

Comeback stories give us second chances. We've all experienced disappointment. When dreams evaporate, tragedy brings us to our knees, loss takes the wind from our spirit. When a momentary lapse in our values, destroys careers. When we, our teams, our organizations, feel stuck, and there just doesn't seem to be a way out. When the hurt of loss — lost jobs, passed-over promotions, fallen-apart big deals, lost relationships, lost family — is a persistent, dull sting. Your workers are either in a storm, coming out of a storm, or will soon hit a storm. About half of new businesses won't survive their first five years and most will fail because of cash flow problems. Fifty percent of employees leave their companies to get away from their toxic bosses. Four in ten workers reported their job was very or extremely stressful. Job stress is more closely associated with health complaints than family or financial problems. Nearly fifteen percent of people had felt like striking a coworker in the past year and forty-two percent report that yelling or other verbal abuse is common. If you don't think your teams have storms in life, just read the newspaper.

Your comeback story will reassure someone — to start on their journey, to finish what they started, to write an unexpected ending to their doleful beginning. Your comeback story — from adversity, from a fall, from despair, from pain, from misfortune, from a failure — marks us and makes us. Your perspective can help others make sense of it all. Leaders are born into unpredictable circumstances, but those circumstances don't define them. What do leaders make of those circumstances? Let your obstacles mean something. Comeback stories teach us that our circumstances — tragic, trying, treacherous — don't make us but can mold us; they don't define our story, certainly not the end to our story. We have the final word.

Types of Comeback stories

The underdog. The unassuming, unexpected hero who falters then succeeds beyond his dreams. There is a little underdog in each of us. Ever been counted out? Did you have a disadvantaged start to your family life, your job, your career? Ever felt average at best? Ever wish someone noticed you, took an interest in you? Ever wish you just were given a shot? We relate to underdogs because we may have been bullied as a child, we may not have had the ideal family circumstances, we may not have been esteemly-educated. The starting circumstances are almost entirely out of our control. We don't choose to be underdogs, but the circumstances plop us there. And it's from there — tragic, troubled, tense circumstances — that underdogs become favorite heroes. When have you been an underdog? Write a story.

Lost and found. We all get a little lost in life — wrong turns, ignorant choices, foolish decisions — but the finding matters most. It's in the gap between lost and found that self-awareness peaks. It is in *becoming* lost and *becoming* found that we grow. When have you been lost and found? Write a story.

Falls, Fails, Fights to Return. When circumstances are bleak, when things begin to crumble, when losses mount, when failure accelerates the decline, some retreat while others fight to return. When have you fought your way back, clawed your way back? Write a story.

Inside You all Along. Sometimes the circumstances bring out hidden traits. We find something inside self. Often, something needed to die — a self-perception, a self-limiting image, a fear. In those moments, we find the truth of who we are — we find the heart of a hero. When have you uncovered something that was burning inside you all along? Write a story.

Best Beats First. Boldness does not always mean first. It doesn't matter who gets there first, so as long as you rally a team to have the courage and determination to find a way to produce a better solution and persevere in continually improving with the belief that good enough never is.

Writing Comeback stories that are Sticky

At the heart of every great comeback story is a tension. The *either…or* decisions that need to be made. The choice to either face it or walk away. The choice to either accept the challenge or give up. In every comeback story is the tension between the old way and the better way. Our brain craves this tension. Hearing the danger, the risk, the doom, the despair, the listener's brain is pumping norepinephrine. Sweaty palms, wide eyes, dilated pupils. Our attention pathway is on full alert. The audience is mirroring the emotional tension of the teller. We've all been there –at the crossroads of choice where *something hangs in the balance.* Let your audience feel it. Give them the room to find it in their past. Let it sink into a distant, but familiar place for them. Don't rush to get to the "good part;" this *is* the good part. When the audience feels, they will empathize. When the audience empathizes, they will connect, they will remember, they will mirror the actions of the comeback hero.

Tension creates the suspense and surprise. Sure, we want the knight to kill the dragon. Sure, we want Rocky to beat Clubber Lang. Sure, we want Elsa to perform an act of true love to thaw a frozen heart. Sure, we want the Apollo 13 astronauts to return to earth.   Sure, we want Sir William Wallace to win his Scottish uprising against King Edward I of England.   Sure, we want to overcome the circumstances in front of us. But before we can overcome the circumstances, we need to overcome something inside us. Something needs to die, perhaps a self-limiting belief. Something needs to change, perhaps a character trait or self-doubt. Becoming antifragile means facing, then overcoming fear — not just through the circumstances, but in ourselves. In those circumstances, we find something deep inside ourselves — maybe something always there but dormant, maybe something hidden until now, maybe something imprinted on you by a role model.

It is the inner transformation that listeners crave.   It's the *But...Then* moment. The turning point. The inner transformation and external turn of events that signal change, deep change, dramatic change, lifelong change. We are anthropologically wired to desire growth — to learn, to stretch, to become better. Better. Better than before.   Better on the other side of the desperate circumstances.   Better on the inside.   That's the power of the comeback story — to foster the inner transformation that is sparked by a belief in better. Something inside us has changed. We learn something about ourselves. Comeback stories re-label us in ways we never could have imagined.

Comeback stories are rarely easy. The irony of becoming the person we want to be, need to be, requires overcoming that which has been steadily denying us.   The things we most fear, most despise, most worry about, most hate become the spark for personal and organizational transformation.   How do you get back up when life gets tough?   When things start to unravel? When the fire seems to have scorched everything?   Courage requires confronting fear.   The most unwanted situations are the catalyst for something beautiful.

Your comeback story will trigger someone else's comeback story. If you want your apprentices to pick themselves up, then you show them what resilience looks like, feels like. You may inspire someone start to moving again after giving up for so long. You may inspire someone to see that their seemingly stalled career isn't the final chapter. You may encourage someone to be the author of their story, not wait for someone else to write it. Everyone needs a comeback at some point or many points in their life. It may indeed start with telling your comeback story.

What is your comeback story?

All of us have one or more than one.

Preparing Your Comeback Story

In your Life Journey Map, what were the difficult choices and transitions you faced? What were those "but...then" defining moments? When did you lean in and really face the tough circumstances? Tell us these stories and what you learned about yourself and others; tell us how those experiences marked you and made you.

Tell us a story about your courage and determination despite desperate circumstances. What are your *Underdog stories, Lost and Found stories, Inside you All Along stories and Fighting to Return stories*?

What are your Come-From-Behind stories? Tell us a story of a time when your resilience or the resilience of your team/organization really surprised you and those around you. What were moments when you were glad you didn't give up, when you decided to persevere?

If I had never experienced _____, then I never would be _____. What are those tense experiences and stories — personally or organizationally — that you shunned at the time, but appreciate today?

Tell us stories about redemption for you or your team, how your starting point didn't define how you finished.

Similar Stories: Goliath-Must-Fall

Your *Goliath-Must-Fall Story* shows us how to overcome

something monolithic, something seemingly insurmountable, something overwhelming that diminishes us yet paradoxically forces us to grow. While it's easy to jump to competitive circumstances metaphorically depicting your Goliath — stalwart industry incumbents, big brands, or oligopolistic companies — clever leaders understand each of us has a Goliath that must fall. For themselves and their teams to become better, we must overcome something inside us, something that holds us back, something that brings out the worst in us, something buried behind the facade. Your stories give others the confidence to face their goliaths.

Preparing Your Goliath-Must-Fall Story

What Goliaths have your team faced? It could be a competitor or competitive circumstance; it could be a business threat, a shutdown, a financial crisis, a quality issue, the loss of a longtime customer, your reputation dragged through the mud. Tell us a story.

What Goliaths are looming in your life and business? Those things that are holding you back, could bring you to your knees, almost taunt you with a control and power over you? Why must your Goliath fall? Tell us stories about how you have overcome the giants in your personal and professional life.

Examples of *Comeback* and *Goliath-Must-Fall* Stories:

Seventy million in forty-two days

Seventy million in forty-two days. They said it couldn't be done — that the biggest product launch of the year needed to be called off, cancelled, costing a write-off of tens of millions of dollars, thousands of retail locations to reset their shelves and damage to our impeccable reputation. When we found *e coli* nearly 45 days into production, the cause unknown, the improbability in a practically dry process... Well, I felt nauseous, a punch in the gut, crushed. Our partner was calling our executives asking for several of us to be fired. But the spirit of this team carried the day. The motto of the Green Berets is, "Improvise, adapt, overcome." We are Production Green Berets. We were only meant to make one million a day — that's what we designed this first-of-a-kind machine to produce. But we found a way to salvage some of what we already produced and make 70 million in 42 days. Through quiet determination, ingenuity and sheer willpower, we overcame the odds and persisted. That moment marked and shaped this team. It impressed something on us that we remember years later, something we'll soon never forget. Devotion at the beginning of a new product is common, but in the face of adversity, persistence is rare. We stayed loyal to something we committed to and we stayed loyal to each other.

Overcoming my fear of speaking

When I was in fourth grade, I had a speech impediment. I could not pronounce correctly words that had an S or an R. Now, there are lots of words in the dictionary using those letters, so you can imagine how frustratingly difficult speaking was for me. When I'd read aloud, I just couldn't make the sounds come out of my mouth fittingly — "R" would come out like "W" and "S" would come out like "TH." Kids laughed at me. You know how mean some can be.

Several times a week, I was excused from class and marshalled to a speech therapist. I didn't feel like I was making progress. Eventually, I avoided speaking altogether because I feared the snickers and eye rolling. I became self-conscious, shy, and withdrawn. When public speaking in front of my class was required for reports, I'd be sleepless for a week. I was miserable. But then in fifth grade I had a teacher. She was actually more than a teacher; she was my encourager. She invited me one day to participate in a public speaking contest. I avoided any direct conversations with her for weeks as the deadline for signing up approached. But she told me how she specifically asked me to represent our school. Dumbfounded, I reluctantly agreed.

I chose a speech by Napoleon, a farewell to his troops — it had the fewest number of R's and S's. We practiced three times a week for several months. Enunciating, gesturing, pausing, pacing. I prayed something, anything would happen so that I wouldn't have to give that speech.

I'll never forget the knotted stomach I had when giving my speech to an audience of parents and evaluators. My dad didn't want to make me more nervous, so he had his head down through my entire speech. When I sat back down next to him, his eyes swelled with tears, and he whispered to me, "Son, I didn't even know that was you. Your booming voice...your speech, your...your words were just perfect." Though I didn't win the speech contest, I won a battle inside of me that day that has carried me through the years. A teacher nudged me to courageously dispel a self-limiting, twisted lie I was telling myself — "not good enough." That day I pulled a label off myself — "can't speak correctly." Find those moments in your life when you feel incapable or incompetent and challenge yourself to overcome your fear. Like my teacher was to me, be a leader that encourages your team by giving them a chance to overcome something or uncover something deep inside themselves.

Best Beats First

I know the news hit us like a brick. They launched before us. It's incredibly disappointing. But it's not time to give up. It's not the end of the story. History is on our side. Google wasn't the first search engine. Starbucks wasn't the first corner coffee shop. Disney was a late entrant in family theme parks. American Express dragged its feet getting into charge-cards. Boeing invested in making the safest, most reliable jets but was slow to launch. IBM didn't have an early lead in computers, neither did Intel in semiconductors nor Wal-Mart with discount retailing. None of them were first, but they were better. Best beats first. Sure they [competitor] launched faster, but we must learn faster. Because the best learner wins. The customer decides who wins, not who goes first. We will win because we will be the best solution. We will find out what they have launched and we have the gift of learning from them so we do it better.

Your *From...To Story* can get your team unstuck, unshackled, unencumbered. Change can be tense, stifling, and paralyzing so these stories instill a pioneering spirit to transform their endeavors and maybe themselves. These stories pull listeners toward a future state by explicitly demonstrating how the status quo is dangerous and what will happen if change isn't embraced. They show the listener why we *must* change. Companies, teams, and people inevitably stall. In aviation the stall point occurs when the pilot loses steering and control of the airplane. To get out of a stall, she needs to point the nose to the ground to obtain enough speed to regain control of the plane. It's counter-intuitive — to advance you need to lean into the thing you are most afraid of. By facing the brutal facts, leaning into their stall by unlearning, and ultimately changing course, listeners find encouragement to take the first few steps in a change journey.

To move them, the story must create a push-and-pull dynamic. It can't be simply a directive. The change, the transition must get personal. The FROM state must feel uncomfortable, anxious, maybe even a little disturbing to push them. The TO state isn't blissful or utopian, but it's better than today; it's full of hope to pull them.

From...To stories trigger a call to arms. They create a sense of urgency to be future focused, not forgetting the past or breaking from the past (your myth of origin matters), but leveraging the past as a springboard for better. If a leader's job is to drive change, then the *From...To* story is one of his or her essential stories.

Preparing Your From...To Stories

From...To stories build bridges so people can span your vision with the current reality. When you write your story, don't get too rational and logical. Bring out the emotion. Let them feel the tension of the past and the hope of the future.

What is your FROM state? It starts by facing the brutal facts. What caused you to be in a stall, a slump, a crisis of confidence? It could be any number of things — missed opportunities, failed launches, strategic missteps, complacency, inertia, a failure of leadership? Let the facts speak for themselves.

What is your TO state? What does it look and feel like? Why is it a better place than..., worth the change from...?

Don't rush to judgement. Deeply listen to the words of customers, suppliers, and employees. Watch behaviors — what is missing in the culture? Are your processes creating rigidities and a check-the-boxes mentality vs. achieving results? Are your strategies predictable and stale? Are you executing with excellence? What is holding you back? Find metaphors that will help you explain the dysfunction and danger of the FROM state. Put it in their language and their terms. Help them see it with fresh eyes.

When did you need to unlearn the past? When your strengths became a weakness, when the routine way of doing things became shackles, when your nimbleness and agility slowly became brittle. Tell us a story about how you overcame it.

When have you been stuck, felt like you were sinking, stifled, boxed-in-a-corner? How did you make the mental and emotional change? What steps did you take? What was the first step — usually the hardest?

When was the current path, the status quo more dangerous than the path toward change? Why did you make the necessary change? What happened? When did you not make the necessary change or waited too long? What happened?

Identify the transformation – your inner transformation and your team/organization's transformation — in FROM/TO parallels. Use examples below to spark ideas for your team's FROM/TO's.

FROM _____ TO _____ Examples:
FROM internal focused TO customer-centric
FROM acting like victims TO creating our own destiny
FROM lots of average initiatives TO fewer, bigger, bolder
FROM making excuses TO taking accountability
FROM playing it safe TO competing to win

Examples of *From...To* Story

We Used to Be Known for Quality

I don't know about you, but few movies move me like *Apollo 13*. When I think about the men and women who rescued those astronauts from certain disaster, I inevitably want to put myself in their shoes. Would I be so ingenious, so persistent, so clever, so uncompromising, so level-headed, so resolute, so brave? Fifty-five hours and fifty-four minutes after launch, after a routine stir of their cryogenic oxygen tanks housed in the cylindrical service module, the *Apollo* crew felt a bang ripple through their spacecraft. A caution and warning light lit up on the control panel. Fourteen minutes later, two oxygen tanks were empty, there was no air, no power, no computer. The acclaimed, unnerving return mission, which gripped the world in April 1970, was described by Commander James Lovell as "a great success in the ability of people to take an almost certain catastrophe and turn it into a successful recovery." We love that part of the story — the improbable return home, the heroes on earth and in space.

Today, I don't want to talk about the magnanimous return. I want to talk about punch-list item 253. After an intensive investigation, the Apollo 13 Accident Review Board identified the cause of the explosion. The post-flight investigation focused on the history of oxygen tank 2, serial number 10024X-TA0009, to explain why it ruptured during a routine procedure. In 1965, the Command Module had undergone many improvements that included raising the permissible voltage to the heaters in the oxygen tanks from 28 to 65 volts DC. Unfortunately, the thermostatic switches on these heaters weren't modified to suit the change. There were 253 quality and safety checks identified during a risk assessment prior to launch. Of those, 252 of the 253 check-list items were verified and assured. Item 253 — check the wiring and thermostatic switches at 65 volts DC for overheating or damage — was not fully assessed. Damaged from eight hours of overheating, the tank was a potential bomb the next time it was filled with oxygen. That bomb exploded on April 13, 1970 — two hundred thousand miles from earth.

What is our number 253? You know that item that gets overlooked, overshadowed by deadlines, shrouded by efficiency, obscured by costs, eclipsed by ignorance. Sure, today we look upon Apollo 13 with words like "our finest hour," but a disaster, a tragedy, a calamity was equally likely and equally avoidable. What is our number 253?

We used to be known for quality. I mean really known for quality. Our HR leaders used to use it as a selling tool to prospective employees from marketing to operations. But something has gotten in the way because we have had a string of too many issues....and we have been generally okay with them. I'm not saying that we wanted them to happen or we condone the oversights and mistakes, but we aren't taking them seriously enough because there is a repetitive pattern. We make exceptions and concessions to the process. All of the boxes don't get checked, double-checked, validated, assured.

What is our number 253? Complete every one of them. Full stop. Leave no stone unturned. Go the extra mile. Check and double-check. If someone says you are being overly cautious, say "not on my watch." Not on our watch.

Climbing Everest

We need a new plan, because our current plan isn't working. We are continuously missing our targets, not because they are inherently wrong, but because we don't have the fundamentals in place to deliver them. We've been trying to climb to the top of Everest too fast.

Today, we have too many fragmented initiatives. What we need is fewer, bigger, bolder bets.

Today, we have plenty of compelling forethought on the "first mile," but mediocre plans to deliver the "last mile" of executional excellence, so our hard work never reaches full potential.

Today, we have a culture of checking the boxes. What we desperately need is a culture that focuses on delivering results not box-checking.

Today, we are difficult to do business with because of the *our way or the highway* attitude, unyielding and maybe a bit arrogant. We put our ideas at the center of everything we do. We need to put the customer at the heart of everything we do.

You don't get to the top of Everest in one climb. You move up the mountain and stop at a series of four camps — always coming back down to Base Camp before moving to the next farther camp. You need a healthy Base Camp to climb to the top of Everest. I don't just mean at the start of the climb, but after every successive Camp as you move up the mountain you come back down to Base Camp. Base Camp is foundational; it's where you recover safely, nourish and prepare for the next big climb. You always come back to Base Camp not in defeat, but in celebration. Going down in elevation feels like defeat, but Base Camp is vital for the head and heart of the climber. So we are re-casting our plans. We are dismantling our undisciplined plans that had us sprinting dangerously to the peak. Instead we are sequentially going to climb Everest by making sure the basics are right at Base Camp while planning for the climb to Camp 1, Camp 2 and so on to the top.

Your *If-Not-You-Then-Who Story* needs to arouse them to heed the call and take action: the call to make things better, the call to say *enough* or *never again*, the call to say *from this day forward*, the call to say *good enough isn't enough*, the call to become the company you once were, the call to stop acting like victims, the call to care deeply about each other, your customers and your clients, the call to believe and act like change agents. In those moments when we can see the problem before anyone else, when we passionately feel like something must be done, when the stakes are high, when seniority and position aren't necessary qualifications to lead the charge, what will you say to inspire co-workers to dive in, to raise their hands, to pick up a shovel and start digging? They might resist — full of self-doubt and short on capability — but they need not feel perfectly prepared. You know they never will if the challenge is steep enough, bold enough, meaningful enough.

It's easy to label ourselves as not-so-brave and not-so-courageous and let ourselves off the hook. Our natural tendency is to wait for the right *if only…if only* our customer or competitor would…, *if only* we had sufficient resources, *if only* the new leadership team would, then…. But waiting for *if only/then* events simply lulls us into a false illusion of being a victim of circumstances, waiting for someone else to give us the green light. So we wander around waiting for those around us or those leading us to give us the okay to take a chance, to make a bold move, to do something important.

Your *If-Not-You-Then-Who Story* emboldens those around us to see what's possible when they can't see it themselves, when they can't see it *in* themselves. They need to hear your story of dying a slow death at work — not physically, but mentally, soulfully — until someone awakened something inside you. That's when you made it personal. That's when you took your turn. They need to hear stories of regret for not heeding the call to transformation, the regret of hiding in the organization waiting until someone else the fix the obvious problems, the deep regret for missed opportunities, the long days, months, years of unnecessary self-talk traps of convincing yourself someone else needed to do something when the truth was you needed to battle your own cowardice. Sure, those stories will require a remarkable portion of vulnerability and bravery. But to wake your team from the trance of complacency, you need to tell about the flourishing you personally experienced from taking the leap or the concealed regret by passing the time. They need to hear that the decision wasn't easy, that you were full of fear and empty of readiness. They need to hear how the least qualified, the imperfectly prepared, the insufficiently talented took a stand, achieved the seemingly impossible and transformed their small part of the world and themselves.

Your *If-Not-You-Then-Who Story* needs to make the call personal. Familiar refrains pepper many water cooler and coffee stations — "I didn't sign up for this," or "it's not my job." Let them hear through your stories how you were glad you raised your hand when no one else did. How you were unprepared but you'll never forget the gripping, heart-pounding, fist-pumping scenes when you were figuratively put on stage. Let them see that they can carve their initials in a bigger story. They need to hear that you carry that experience in your pocket today and how it shaped you for things to come.

Similar Stories: It's-Your-Turn and Because-Only-You-Can

It's-Your-Turn Story will enable you to inspire your apprentices when it's their turn…to lead, to push for better, for disruptive, for unconventional, to continue even if the answers aren't clear and the work is rough, to encourage them to stop waiting for someone else to make the first move, but instead be the person who makes the change. Show them through your stories that you always have the opportunity to build something lasting, something worth contributing to, something legacy-worthy, and that you don't have to wait for the opportunity to be given to you. Because when you see something that aches you, rubs you, infuriates you, impassions you, then it's personal, and it's your turn. They need to hear from you that they don't need permission to take their turn. That they only need to have a little audacity.

Because-Only-You-Can Story. Your team members and apprentices need the encouragement to go without being ready. They need an internal narrative sparked and nurtured by you that calls them to greatness at the intersection of what they are deeply passionate about, their unique strengths, and what the world needs. Let them see that they are uniquely gifted to take ahold of a tough challenge. Let them see generosity of a different kind — to offer themselves as change agents in their communities, organizations, teams, not for self-aggrandizement but in service to others. Let your stories help them to see this as the chance of a lifetime, their lifetime. Not someone else's. Not later. Now.

Preparing Your *If-Not-You-Then-Who* Stories

When have you faced into change – personal, team, or organizational change — and when have you chosen not to? What lessons, wisdom, regrets, and rewards can you share?

When have you gone without being ready, imperfectly prepared or first without knowing what's coming next? What did you learn about yourself? How did the experience change you?

When have you felt like the circumstances demanded something more from you — not because you were better but because you cared, you were committed, you were passionate? Circumstances when you felt like it was your turn to lead? When did you raise your hand when no one else did and you were so glad that you did? Any "turns" you wish you'd taken but instead passed on?

Examples of *If-Not-You-Then-Who, It's-Your-Turn, Because-Only-You-Can* stories:

Hold the rope
You are holding a rope here today because the rope holds significance for us.

Grab it with both hands. Look around this office — hundreds of feet of rope binding us together. All of us holding this piece of rope.

When you climb K2 or Everest, you tie a rope around each other — so no one is lost. If you can't see through the blinding blizzard, you trust the rope. The rope is your assurance because someone ahead of you is setting the course and taking the first steps of danger.

When you are weathering a storm at sea, when the wind and rain come rolling through, when the boat can easily get swept away, tossed to and fro, you drop an anchor with a rope. The rope is your security, holds you steady, anchors you in.

When someone is drowning, gasping for air, desperate for help, you throw a rope. The rope is your life saver.

When you rock climb, when your next move might be a fall hundreds of feet to your peril, someone knots you in, harnesses you with them — so you are in it together. The rope is your confidence. The rope allows you to move up, to move on, to move higher, to move together.

If the rope could speak, it would say, "I've got you." And it would say that over and over again. I've got you. I've got you. I've got you.

Ropes are made from tiny strands of fibers — weak by themselves, but strong when woven, bound, working together. Somehow, we've lost that along the way. I've lost that along the way. We've stopped working together as a team and started going it alone; we've stopped helping each other and started finger-pointing when problems arise. We've let the rope fray for too long. When the time to delivery started slipping for Project Abacus, we dropped the rope, I dropped the rope.

You can't push a rope, you can only pull it. Somehow we've lost that along the way. I've lost that along the way. We've been pushing so hard, so far — pushing the results, pushing each other. It's gotten the best of us. Instead of pulling each other, we've been fruitlessly pushing each other.

I'm convinced the reason why we are stalled — why the growth hasn't come like we wanted it to — has less to do with our strategy and more to do with us and this rope. To become bigger on the outside, we need to go to work on the inside. It starts with me because I haven't been setting a very good example with my leadership team.

So today, it's our turn to hold the rope – together. We are going to stop using the rope in a tug-of-war with each other and start using it to run a three-legged race — with arms around each other and bound together. Today, it's our turn to hold the rope...to anchor in with the rope; we are going to pull each other up the mountain with the rope; we are going to save each other with the rope.

We Need to Own This

We need to attack this service quality problem that is blemishing our brand and tarnishing our reputation. We need to take this personally. We need fresh eyes and a heart for change.

For the last decade, more people have died from hospital acquired infections then breast cancer! These are unintentional human-errors made in the hospital: poorly washed hands, unsanitized skin, unclean rooms, unsanitized equipment and medical devices. For years, these were generally accepted as risks in hospital procedures and stays. Think about it – one million people get a hospital acquired infection every year from an error. Brave hospital personnel started seeing these problems with fresh eyes; they started seeing that these are preventable risks not inevitable risks. On the leading edge, like every major rebellion, were the revolutionaries. They looked to the airline industry as a role model, where like the medical profession, millions of people rely on their safety every day. Decades ago, plane crashes were an inevitable risk until they instituted systemic change in the form of something simple, yet profound — checklists. Dr. Atul Gwande has called it *The Checklist Manifesto* — a call for hospitals to systematize procedures into simple checklists. Some hospitals have used checklists to create not only reliability, but also a culture change, because they put something at stake — lives, their reputation, their integrity. Some hospitals haven't had any hospital-acquired infections for several years. Fresh eyes, a commitment to change, a systematized approach.

We need to take this service quality issue we are having personally — each of us individually, all of us collectively. Something very real is at stake — our reputation and our livelihood. Customers are leaving us because they are frustrated, because they can't get answers, because we aren't very responsive. It looks to them that we aren't taking it seriously, and they have lost patience, confidence, and trust in us. Who has ever called for service work at their home, waiting all day for someone to show, only to have them cancel? We are acting like that right now. Who has ever been frustrated with the purchase of an automobile or appliance, a big ticket item — only to have it break or fail way too soon with the manufacturer hiding behind the warranty legalese? How did that feel? That's how our customers feel. Who has ever called a help desk only to have them unhelpful? Did you feel helpless, frustrated, angry? It is to our customers and it needs to be for us.

You are Preventionists

This is the only place in the US where a study like this happened. This little skilled nursing facility tucked away in rural Pennsylvania has taught us something remarkable — some of the most prevalent illnesses that debilitate the aged are largely preventable and not as some think inevitable. When flu hit near epidemic levels this year and facilities across this state and in this county had to close their doors to new residents, this facility didn't. Public health officials wanted to know why. Through your teamwork – monitoring patients more closely, washing hands and surfaces more thoroughly, analyzing patient data and looking for patterns, making sure elders washed their hands after toileting, before and after eating, making sure family sanitized hands before social events – you have cut the chain of transmission and subsequently the incidence of pneumonia, respiratory infections, norovirus, the flu by nearly sixty percent. You have prevented dozens of elders from getting sick and maybe even dying. Now it's time for you to continue without us. Now it's time for you to train new staff members, educate new elders and their families, continue to advance the study of preventing communicable disease transmission in skilled nursing facilities. Because only you can advance the cause. Because only you can keep keep learning and discovering new, practical ways to break the cycle of infection. Doctors diagnose, nurses treat, caregivers prevent. You aren't just caregivers. You are preventionists.

Your *What If...Vision* Story

Your *What-if Story* instills a pioneering spirit. It creates a gravitational pull toward an inspiring, hopeful vision. When you open windows of curiosity for your people to see with a new perspective, you enhance their ability to imagine a different future. Your *What-if Stories* create vivid images of what the future may hold. Your team can't quite describe it, but you help them to see it with your stories. Your team can't plan for it, but you can help them feel it — a vision too big to fit in their head, but one that can fit in their hearts.

So many of our projects don't resemble our original vision, so we give up our dreams early. You don't invent the dream; it's already inside you, it's already inside your team. The dream doesn't die, it just gets buried underneath layers of responsibilities and well-intentioned tasks, to-do lists and annual objectives. Your *What-If* Story jolts your team into jettisoning mediocre expectations and encourages them to tap into their greatness and longingly wonder what could be. Your stories can propel them to start believing again, to help them see that they have enough to get started by looking with fresh eyes at what they have to work with. To imagine starting something that they may never see finished...the great unfinished work, an endeavor so grand that others need to be inspired to finish it. It can be thrilling and even more exciting than a finished work. Sometimes the unfinished works of great thinkers have the potential to be their greatest works. During the 16th Century, Leonardo da Vinci and Michelangelo, both left so many works of their art unfinished that became popular for artists to try to achieve unfinished effects. There is even an Italian term for this style: *non finito*.

What-if Stories summon people to dream, to embrace the beautiful constraints of their current state and use whatever they have as a fulcrum to begin building. They follow you not because they know exactly where you are taking them, but because you and your vision are worth following.

One rupee a day

Some of you have said that I'm different coming back from my trip to India – determined, headstrong, fiery. I want you to understand where that passion is coming from. The first evening I returned to my hotel room from the villages I fell to the floor and sobbed. After spending the day visiting the rural villages where our water filters will be used, I was drained of emotion. I've never witnessed poverty, destitution, like this. Open defecation, open urination. No running water. Kids missing school because they were unnecessarily sick. Adults missing work because they were unnecessarily sick — no sick days, just no money that day and therefore, maybe no food.

This project doesn't just provide clean water, it promotes economic and social development. Clean water is a multiplier. What if our filter provided more than clean water: what if it could promote wellness, what if it financially helped impoverished families from missing work, what if it supported a child's education by preventing sick kids from missing school. What if what we worked on provided hope – how many times in our life will have this opportunity? I know we have reached some barriers and detours in our development, but we must find a way. I know one rupee a day for clean water feels insurmountable, but we must find a way.

Similar Stories: Undiscovered-Country

Our team, our organizations, our endeavors have a persistent inner voice that beacons us to a far-off land. The pioneering spirit of invention, of resolving injustice, of 'white space' invites us to the edge. Personal and organizational growth happens at the edge. Expansion happens at the edge. Hope happens at the edge.

When John F. Kennedy became President in January 1961, many Americans considered the United States significantly behind the Russians in the space race. Almost four years earlier, Russia's *Sputnik 1* was the first satellite launched into space and just a few months after Kennedy's inauguration, the Russians launched the first man into space. NASA administrator James Webb, told the President that there was little to no chance of beating the Russians on launching a laboratory space station, but with a significant investment ($22 billion) and resolve, the US could land a man on the moon and return him safely before 1970. The commitment was audacious and bold, daring and inspiring because so much was unknown — new heat-tolerant materials needed to be invented, new energy supplies and new water filtration technologies needed to be developed, new cooling suits needed to be created, new food preservation methods needed to be conceived.

In a visit to Houston in September of 1962, Kennedy delivered a rousing speech before a crowd at Rice University that inspired the nation. In this excellent example of an *Undiscovered-Country* story, Kennedy characterized space as a beckoning frontier, provoking the pioneering spirit of America that has prevailed since its founding. He invited us to share in a collective vision with hope, possibility, and a sense of urgency.

Here is an excerpt:

> We set sail on this new sea because there is new knowledge to be gained, and new rights to be won, and they must be won and used for the progress of all people. For space science, like nuclear science and all technology, has no conscience of its own. Whether it will become a force for good or ill depends on man, and only if the United States occupies a position of pre-eminence can we help decide whether this new ocean will be a sea of peace or a new terrifying theater of war. I do not say that we should or will go unprotected against the hostile misuse of space any more than we go unprotected against the hostile use of land or sea, but I do say that space can be explored and mastered without feeding the fires of war, without repeating the mistakes that man has made in extending his writ around this globe of ours.
>
> There is no strife, no prejudice, no national conflict in outer space as yet. Its hazards are hostile to us all. Its conquest deserves the best of all mankind, and its opportunity for peaceful cooperation may never come again. But why, some say, the Moon? Why choose this as our goal? And they may well ask, why climb the highest mountain? Why, thirty-five years ago, fly the Atlantic? Why does Rice play Texas?
>
> We choose to go to the Moon! We choose to go to the Moon in this decade and do the other things, not because they are easy, but because they are hard; because that goal will serve to organize and measure the best of our energies and skills; because that challenge is one that we are willing to accept, one we are unwilling to postpone, and one we intend to win, and the others, too.

Preparing your *What-if* Stories

What vision do you need to create so others see the future with a fresh, audacious perspective?

What dreams for the future do you hold in your head or heart that need to be shared with your team?

What hopeful possibilities does you need your team to see, imagine, start preparing for where the end is clear, but the means might not be neatly understood? How can you prepare them to go without being ready?

What is the undiscovered country for your team or organization?

Example of *What-if and Undiscovered-Country* Stories:

Playing Four Hands of Piano with Ten Fingers

Art Tatum was one of America's greatest jazz pianists. Art Tatum was legally blind. He was senselessly and tragically beaten as a young boy which caused him to lose much of his vision. But Art dreamed of playing the piano. Economically disadvantaged, Art couldn't afford piano lessons. That didn't hold him back. He would go into town and ask someone to hold his hand, orienting him to the saloon. Someone would walk him toward the back where he would place his hands on the keys of the player piano and learn to play by feeling the keys and listening for the notes. Night after night this was how practically blind Art Tatum learned how to play the piano.

What Art did not know at the time was that the player piano manufacturers used two pianists on some of the music. So Art Tatum learned how to play four hands of piano with his ten fingers. He did what no one thought was possible. Isn't it likely that if Art knew he would need to learn to play four hands of piano with only his tem fingers, he may never have tried.

Oh, the power of limitations. Art's blindness, his poverty, his naiveté created a beautiful constraint and allowed him to break a paradigm. His misfortune gave him an advantage. The beginning of his story didn't define the end of his story.

Embrace the power of limitations. There is no question that some of our launches in our strategic plan require an invention, a massive breakthrough that hasn't been done before. But we are starting a journey to reclaim our rightful role as leaders in our market, the market we created through ingenuity and first-in-the-world product launches. Recently we have relinquished that leadership to other companies; we are going to get it back. Sure, we don't have the resourcing we used to. But I want you to believe in the power of limitations like Art Tatum. Sure, we don't have everything we need. But we do have curiosity, determination, a winning spirit and the power to overcome our self-imposed limitations.

Stories that teach and apprentice
Your *Let-Me-Tell-You-What ___ Looks-Like Story*

Your *Let-Me-Tell-You-What ___ Looks-Like* Story brings your values to life. Mission statements and corporate values are empty words hung in lobbies without stories. There is a vast divide between the definition of values and principles laminated on cards and seeing them in action. To believe in your organizational values, to want them embedded in the fabric of your organization, to witness them played out unprompted, then you need to search for evidence of them being lived out. You can tell people about putting the "customer at the center of everything we do" or you can tell a story about a sales rep who pulled an all-nighter helping a customer prepare for an important presentation to her CEO. You can tell people that you value "transparency and honesty" or you can tell a story about how gossip and backbiting nearly destroyed your organization, how people turned on each other rather than the enemy in the marketplace. Stories can honor the values that you cherish in your company or team, and they can also be the spark for showcasing behaviors that need to be crystallized to make a step-change in cultural transformation. For a team that needs to take risks and move faster with incomplete information, tell a *Let Me Tell You What Agility Looks Like* story. For a team that needs an unwavering re-commitment to quality, then tell a *Let Me Tell You What a "Never Again" Commitment to Quality Looks Like* story. For a team that needs to move from "me" to "we," tell a *Let Me Tell You What Mutual Accountability Looks Like* story.

Storytelling allows our values to creep into the relevance of our everyday work lives not through rules but through relationships. When story is the currency in organizations, employees aspire to stalwart character traits and shudder at the consequences of integrity-compromising decisions. They want to live up to the stories that are told. Through stories, team and organizational values come to life — how boldness and determination not resources propels initiatives; how putting the customer first doesn't always mean you are last; how caring prevails, but not usually in the way we imagine. Through stories, every day heroes emerge in the front-lines of our organizations, the unsung heroes of customer service and payroll, the forgotten heroes on our manufacturing lines and warehouses.

If you want people to live out the values you hold so dear, then you need to give them role models through stories. Values drive decisions, and decisions drive outcomes. If you want to change your outcomes, you need to do more than change your decisions, you need to change belief in your values. Many companies have run aground in the seemingly superficiality of poor management decisions only to uncover the frayed knots of values unravelling. Many corporate turnarounds — from Ford to Delta Airlines, Apple to Starbucks — centered on reinvigorating core values. Core value statements can't change behaviors and beliefs. Stories can. If you want behaviors repeated over and over again, then tell people the stories that reinforce those behaviors. Let them see real examples of ethics in action, values under threat, principles played out at their best.

Overtly notice value-based behaviors you want repeated again — name the label and affix it on people and teams so they wear it proudly for others to follow. They will wear the label again, and they will want to live up to the label affixed to them so they are consistent with its real and figurative meaning. These stories prompt your team to see the everyday events in their work lives not just as random circumstances, but as extraordinary opportunities to place their fingerprints, to touch with a silver lining, to make a difference in the lives of customers and co-workers. Let them see you cheering them on. Let them know that you believe in them. Let your organization know that your values matter; they are powerful.

Let-Me-Tell-You-What ____ *Looks-Like* Stories create legends in organizations. Our stories can develop the core narratives for our company, our teams, and our employees. Stories can create positive self-perceptions for beleaguered teams that can overcome stigmas. Apprentices and teams will live up to the stories told about them. They will live up to the qualities we admire in them. Stories elevate the performance of everyone who hears them.

Let Me Tell You What FOCUS Looks Like

Six months ago, we realized that our lack of focus was causing us to deliver mediocre results. Our intention was right, but we were exhausted from numerous initiatives desperately trying to get us financially and strategically back on track. We have a culture that rewards us to do MORE; it's like a badge of honor. More projects, more hours, more busyness. But we need to do LESS. It's not easy. To redirect people and projects mid-year is complex. But this team came together and took the first stab at making *Focus* a reality; they took the number of active projects down from 39 to 17. Some people's feelings were hurt, some people raised hell over it, some leaders had their projects pushed forward another year. Tough decisions were made. If this company wants to know what the dividends of Focus looks like – here it is. More products will be launched on-time and on-budget next year than any of the last five.

Let Me Tell You What CUSTOMER DELIGHT Looks Like

I received a wonderful note from a guest last week. He praised one of our employees, Sandy. He said what she did was "one of the rarest acts of sincere kindness I've experienced from a stranger and the most extraordinary experience I've received at a hotel." At check-in, Sandy asked how long he'll be staying in Hong Kong and he described only a few days. He mentioned worrying about not having enough time to get his son a present from Hong Kong, asking Sandy for directions to local shopping. She noticed for the next few days that he was working very late. After the first night, she asked if he had enjoyed any local food favorites. He said he'd been working all day in a conference room, and didn't get a chance to eat anything local. The next night when he arrived in his hotel room late, there was an egg tart; the night after that mango sago pomelo pudding waiting for him in his room. The day before he left, he asked how late the souvenir shops were open. She noticed he arrived back to the hotel very late that evening with nothing more than a briefcase. The next day Sandy purchased and wrapped a small gift for his son and arranged for the concierge to give it to him when he returned back to the hotel to retrieve his luggage before heading to the airport. Imagine to his surprise, arriving back to the hotel to grab his bags and rush to the airport, only to find a kind note saying how Sandy wanted him to take home a little bit of Hong Kong to his son. This is what "delighting our customers" looks like. Listening intently, noticing, anticipating and then doing something kind. Sandy, thank you for showing us what extraordinary guest service and what delighting the customer looks like.

Similar Stories: What-We-Have-Learned

Your *What-We-Have-Learned* Story codifies wisdom, experience, and lessons so people and teams are accumulating learning and through the DNA of success and mistakes alike. In the hyper-paced workplace, it's easy to miss the significance of slowing down and focusing on learning to build capability. Stories, more than decks and fact books, propel capability and professional enlightenment.

When JK Rowling, famed author of the *Harry Potter* series, addressed the Harvard Class of 2008 in her unguarded and moving Commencement speech, she provided the gift of battle-tested life sagacity and undisguised stance on failure. Here is a portion of her speech:

On this wonderful day when we are gathered together to celebrate your academic success, I have decided to talk to you about the benefits of failure. And as you stand on the threshold of what is sometimes called "real life," I want to extol the crucial importance of imagination.

These may seem quixotic or paradoxical choices, but please bear with me.

I am not dull enough to suppose that because you are young, gifted, and well-educated, you have never known hardship or heartbreak. Talent and intelligence never yet inoculated anyone against the caprice of the Fates, and I do not for a moment suppose that everyone here has enjoyed an existence of unruffled privilege and contentment.

However, the fact that you are graduating from Harvard suggests that you are not very well-acquainted with failure. You might be driven by a fear of failure quite as much as a desire for success. Indeed, your conception of failure might not be too far from the average person's idea of success, so high have you already flown.

Ultimately, we all have to decide for ourselves what constitutes failure, but the world is quite eager to give you a set of criteria if you let it. So, I think it fair to say that by any conventional measure, a mere seven years after my graduation day, I had failed on an epic scale. An exceptionally short-lived marriage had imploded, and I was jobless, a lone parent, and as poor as it is possible to be in modern Britain without being homeless. The fears that my parents had had for me, and that I had had for myself, had both come to pass, and, by every usual standard, I was the biggest failure I knew.

Now, I am not going to stand here and tell you that failure is fun. That period of my life was a dark one, and I had no idea that there was going to be what the press has since represented as a kind of fairy tale resolution. I had no idea then how far the tunnel extended, and for a long time, any light at the end of it was a hope rather than a reality.

So why do I talk about the benefits of failure? Simply because failure meant a stripping away of the inessential. I stopped pretending to myself that I was anything other than what I was, and began to direct all my energy into finishing the only work that mattered to me. Had I really succeeded at anything else, I might never have found the determination to succeed in the one arena I believed I truly belonged. I was set free, because my greatest fear had been realized, and I was still alive, and I still had a daughter whom I adored, and I had an old typewriter and a big idea. And so rock bottom became the solid foundation on which I rebuilt my life.

You might never fail on the scale I did, but some failure in life is inevitable. It is impossible to live without failing at something, unless you live so cautiously that you might as well not have lived at all — in which case, you fail by default.

Failure gave me an inner security that I had never attained by passing examinations. Failure taught me things about myself that I could have learned no other way. I discovered that I had a strong will, and more discipline than I had suspected; I also found out that I had friends whose value was truly above the price of rubies.

The knowledge that you have emerged wiser and stronger from setbacks means that you are, ever after, secure in your ability to survive. You will never truly know yourself, or the strength of your relationships, until both have been tested by adversity. Such knowledge is a true gift, for all that it is painfully won, and it has been worth more than any qualification I ever earned.

So, given a Time Turner, I would tell my twenty-one-year-old self that personal happiness lies in knowing that life is not a check-list of acquisition or achievement. Your qualifications, your CV, are not your life, though you will meet many people of my age and older who confuse the two. Life is difficult, and complicated, and beyond anyone's total control, and the humility to know that will enable you to survive its vicissitudes.

Similar Stories: Your Gratitude Story

Your *Gratitude Story* shares your deep appreciation for the often-unnoticed acts of kindness, conviction, dedication, and sacrifice from individuals and teams. Gratitude can be contemporary — recognizing people and teams for their outstanding contribution. Gratitude can also be retrospective — acknowledging mentors, leaders, and peers for forming and shaping you, imprinting traits and lessons, carrying you or caring for you, believing in you.

Thanksgiving

My wife and I were newlyweds when I started my summer internship during graduate school (in a city ten hours away by car or an expensive plane ticket), and it was really taking its toll on our marriage. We were both miserable and lonely. The vice president of the company I worked for came to see me one day and asked how I was doing. I was excited to share the work I had been doing over the summer, but she could sense something wasn't right with me. "Are you okay, because the joy and smile you had when you started here...well, I'm just not seeing it." Tearing up, I told her about how my wife and I weren't doing well. "Let's see how we can help," she said. The next day flowers arrived at my wife's apartment along with a plane ticket her to visit, concert tickets and restaurant reservations with gift cards. Enclosed was a beautiful, empathetic note to my wife from the VP. The note didn't make us feel awkward, but told us she understood because she had been there too. It was more than touching; it was heartfelt and real. It was personal.

If you want to know why I send notes to your families every year at Thanksgiving — thanking them for sharing you, for the long nights, travel away from them — it's because I know how it feels. I want them to know that they matter to us, because they matter to you.

What values and beliefs does your organization or team hold sacrosanct?   What values are the glue that holds your organization together, that distinguishes your culture from others, that isn't easily replicated by competitors?

Our organization/team always . . . {Fill in the blank — makes and keeps promises? Puts others before self? Respects and honors all people? Is positive and encouraging no matter the circumstances? Is resourceful and never wasteful? Will persevere? Has a can-do attitude and is imaginative?}

Our organization/team is never .... {Fill in the blank — Complacent? Too busy to help? Arrogant? Short-sighted?}

What are some stories that can inspire your organization to remain steadfast and resolute to these values when they will be called on in crisis, when their relevance will be scrutinized, when shades of gray will test them?

Re-tell some life experiences when you were tested, vulnerable, shaken, but your unfaltering values, implacable character, or faithfulness to your beliefs prevailed.

What values and beliefs do you need to intentionally imprint in your teams and organization? What negative behaviors have you unintentionally imprinted?   Make two columns — one for behaviors you want to imprint and one for questionable behaviors you may be unintentionally imprinting, and then list as many of each. Be authentic and vulnerable in order to truthfully depict the desired characteristics as well as the dark side of behaviors you want to start dismantling.

What positive prompts do your team, team members, mentees need to hear from you? Tell them in a story about a time when they impressed you, wow'ed you, taught you something, or made a mark on you.

Think about mentors and master builder, exceptional leaders and co-workers. Write a gratitude story when they made a deep impression on you. Send it to them.

Examples of *Let-Me-Tell-You-What ___ Looks-Like Story, Gratitude Story, What-We-Have-Learned Story*

Let Me Tell You What THINK CUSTOMER Looks Like

When you put the customer at the center of everything you do, great things happen. They may not be immediate, they may not always be intuitive, but great things eventually happen. When Dale got a call from one of his customers asking for his help preparing for a presentation to his boss, Dale was there the same day. Dale was trusted by this customer as someone objective, smart and "good with numbers and PowerPoint." So Dale helped him prepare for his annual budget — only a small bit which was anything about our products. Dale spent the better part of the day with him — postponing reports he was to deliver and team meetings he was to attend — helping his customer prepare for the tense and difficult budget request and capital spending he desperately needed. Of all his suppliers, he trusted Dale. About a month later I received a call from this customer applauding Dale. Let me paraphrase what he said: *as long as Dale is around, I'll be buying from you...even though I know I'm paying as much as 10% more – I'm getting so much more out of our partnership.*

Gratitude Story

Few things are more painful as restructurings. Last month was particularly painful for me, for us. As we watched some of our colleagues leave, some friends move on; it was hard. But Maria put her arms around those effected and gave them hope. She made time to meet with some of them over and over again, helping with their resumes, their benefits, their job prospects. She was on the phone at night, sometimes over coffee on the weekend, sometimes just holding hands and hearing people vent. I received this letter from someone who had been let go; let me read it.

"Nothing prepares you for losing your job. It felt like a punch in the stomach. I was embarrassed to tell my family. All I could hear was "we don't want you anymore." That's not what anyone was really saying, but that's what I was feeling and it just flattened me. That's until Maria came alongside me — she was my encourager, my life coach, my confidant, my resume builder. Dark days and lonely nights were better because of her — she'd reach out after hours to check on me. Kindness and respect aren't just words on the wall in that building (that I'll miss). They are lived out through great people — remember that long after I'm gone— I know I will."

What Maria has shown us is that we can never be too busy to be caring.

Your *Defining Moment Story.*

Your *Defining Moment* Stories imprint wisdom and lessons at critical junctures when much is on the line. These stories provide cautionary lessons that can derail even the most stalwart leader, accomplished apprentice or exceptional team. These stories provide guardrails — alerting people and teams before impending danger to keep us from catastrophe. These stories encourage us to keep moving when we can't see the terrain ahead. These heartfelt and often vulnerable stories teach us what you learned along the way — the regretful, searing lessons and the glorious achievements. These stories teach many through the experience of one. What crossroads will they inevitably face? How can you give them an advantage — not by making the decision for them but by providing the gift of hindsight and foresight for them to make better decisions?

More than binary right-or-wrong stories, *Defining Moment* Stories provide a perspective by living in your shoes. Defining moments aren't about you giving them rational arguments to consider. The team has already poured over the spreadsheets, the scenario-planning is coming up ambivalent, your team is split. They need your prudence and prescience, far-sightedness and forethought. They need your perspective. The perspective that comes from the keen gift of contemplation, hindsight and experience. If you want to impress upon your high potential apprentice the significance of having impeccable professional integrity, you can tell them a story about a time when bonus-on-the-line, you placed your personal interest above your company's most valued, long-standing customer only to have them leave shortly thereafter, in the wake leaving a gaping hole in your company's revenue as well as stinging personal embarrassment. Defining moments are pivots, fulcrums, turning points. Something hangs in the balance. We often can't see it. Legacy leaders freely offer the cherished gift of sound discernment amid the storm of emotions swirling around life's toughest choices, crossroads, forks-in-the-road. What took you a lifetime to learn that you don't want them to take a lifetime to learn?

Organizations have *Defining Moment* Stories too. These elemental building blocks expose the mindset of how your organization deals with change, with success and devastation, with values-at-the-expense-of-results tradeoffs. They embolden us not with pithy sayings or overused maxims, but with up-close, raw, in-the-moment intentions and actions. We have the privilege of leveraging hindsight to become out foresight. We witness the challenges overcome, the tense choices made, the ramifications projected years, maybe decades later. If you want to impress upon your employees the significance of quality, you can have them see the progress against your key performance indicators over the years or you can tell them a story about a time when some sloppy mistakes, some passivity to following up with apparent outlier risks, some complacency in alerting the authorities, nearly escalated to a recall that could have brought your company to its knees in financial costs and brand ruin.

Every legacy leader has defining moments. Moments that shape and change us. Moments of left and right turns. These moments aren't easy to recognize when you're experiencing them. Invariably, we don't appreciate their significance. They feel like a blur. But as you look back, you can recognize the small twists and turns that have shaped you. Sometimes even the most tense or embarrassing become glorious moments. They aren't just meant for you. When we tell a story, we pay forward the lesson.

Sallie Krawcheck's Defining Moment

Sallie Krawcheck, Chair of Ellevate Asset Management, faced a defining moment only weeks after joining Merrill Lynch as a senior leader in the wealth management division. The Stable Value fund, invested in by hundreds of thousands of people, particularly low-income earners, had lost value because the team had mismanaged the money into higher risk investments. Wal-Mart was the biggest owner of the Stable Value Fund as many employees invested part of their retirement savings plan in an investment that they thought could not be lost. What was worse, Sallie had been fired from Citigroup's wealth management years earlier for reimbursing clients for their losses in investments. "I'd lost my job once for doing this...did I want to do it again? And the answer is, I did. There wasn't a lot of sleepless nights. In a way, I had set a precedent for myself on this. I set a precedent...that I was willing to lose my job for it." (Giang, 2015)

Moments are powerful. Moments come in all forms.

Moments of transformation. Mountains and valleys. Turning points and pivots. Boundary markers that separate the old from new, before and after. What circumstances — those tense, sometimes tragic circumstances, desperately unwanted and almost always unwelcome — unleashed something beautiful, something hidden inside you. What rare traits — courage, fortitude, persistence, will, steadfastness, raw honesty, resilience — sprung like a well when the stressful circumstances elicited a new you? What circumstances illuminated your giftedness in a way that surprised you.

Moments of honor. Conquering challenges. Positive moments that shape our self-esteem. Moments that marked you and your organization. What words spoken about you have brought you a deep sense of pride, when you saw yourself differently, through the eyes of someone else, when the recognition felt personal? When was it more than simple pride and feeling appreciated but, a defining moment in self-reflection, self-realization, or self-confidence?

Moments of insight. A-ha moments of learning. When has wisdom been illuminated through the fog of confusing circumstances? When have experience and good judgement, sagacity and acumen won the day over intelligence? When has prudence and perception cut through the clutter of emotions to help you or others see clearly? When have you sensed you were on the wrong path and that you needed to turn around, admit a mistake and move on?

Moments of bonding. When has individuality yielded to collectivity? When has a shared sense of purpose connected people together in ways unforeseen? When has a shared struggle brought people together to lean on each other, to lend a hand to each other, to support and help each other in a dramatic way that jumpstarted new ways of working?

Legacy leaders can sense defining moments in foresight, not just hindsight. They can even create moments that are markers, signposts, flags-in-the-ground. They are purposeful creators of moments. They know when apprentices will uncover a hidden trait and grow; they appreciate when teams will pivot and come up stronger; they discern when organizations need to break from the past. They know how to make even the most haphazard, seemingly inconsequential moments mean something.

We need to be ready for those moments when our leadership is on the line. Maybe only a few people will be touched by our decisions, or maybe many will, but we need to be prepared to seize the opportunity. In those moments, we need to understand that there is more on the line than the immediate decision with weighty consequences. What have you been willing to sacrifice for, take risks for, stand alone for? Those moments when something is on the line — your reputation, your livelihood, your brand reputation, your credentials, your values, your security — you learn something about yourself. We don't want to pass uncertainty down to our team; we want to pass growth-enabling stories. Those moments have the pivotal potential to imprint something deeply meaningful and lasting, a catalyst that can become the first domino. We need to ask, *what is the most enduring lesson for my actions now?* Legacy leaders create enduring moments of meaning. Find yours and create them for others.

Your team will long remember your *Defining Moment* Story when they are faced with one. In those moments, you want them to ask silently, confidently to themselves, "What story do I want to tell?" They will know something hangs in the balance. They will prepare the story to be told from the ending backwards.

Similar Stories: Leap-and-Climb Story

There are stories when you need team members to remove self-doubt and take a leap of faith and start the rigorous climb; when they are worried about falling from the leap of faith, how they are seen, how they might be rejected, they need to know from your story that it's worth it. It's worth the risk.

It's easy for them to sense the pain of failure in that moment of leap. Have them feel the pain of not reaching their potential, the pain of never trying, the pain of giving up too early, the pain of missing the opportunity to make a difference. It's so much easier to stay where we are than to take to a leap, than to stay on the path of simply doing what we are told and ensuring we are accepted because there isn't anything that feels worse than being unprepared. If they wait until they are adequately prepared, then they will never take a leap. The leap requires faith and that faith may come from your story. Then there's the climb.

When have you taken a leap, taken a chance on someone, made a jump into a new career or endeavor? When have you put something on the line — not with Vegas-style gambling, but with self-assurance and conviction?

Some of our apprentices are walking around with tape measures and scales. We fear not being good enough, and that fear keeps us from living our full potential. The constant questions — *Do I measure up? Am I good enough?* — they keep us from trying.

Preparing Your *Defining Moments* and *Leap-and-Climb* Stories

Think about the defining moments in your life that marked you, made you. What moments have marked your team and your organization — moments of honor, moments of insight, moments of bonding, moments of transformation in your apprentices, your teams, your organization? What hung in the balance? What can you see more clearly now with twenty-twenty hindsight that wasn't so apparent at the time?

Tell a positive defining moment story — when you made a really good decision that wasn't so easy. What lesson can your listeners and apprentices learn from you?

Tell a negative defining moment story. What poor decision did you make at a critical juncture? What were the lessons?

What *Defining Moment* Stories exist in your company or organization? What hung in the balance of those tough choices, or what circumstances were thrust on the organization? Why did this story mark the organization "from this day forward?" How have you seen it play out?

Examples of *Defining Moments* and *Leap-and-Climb* Stories

Getting Called out of the Classroom

I was called out of class unexpectedly. The "ohhhh's" from my classmates made my face beet red. I didn't think I had done anything wrong — I was a pretty straight-and-narrow teen — with a few left turns here and there — but today I couldn't recall anything that I'd done that wrong. I mean something that would warrant a call to the principal's office. What I heard was, "Your dad has been in an accident at work; he's in the hospital. Your aunt is coming to get you. I'm so sorry. It's bad, real bad. Oh, sweetie. I'm so sorry." The secretary's eyes filled with tears, and my worry turned to fear.

My invincible dad, this giant of a man, my hero, never fully recovered from an unfortunate forklift accident at work caused by rushing people pushing against deadlines. A silly mistake turned into a tragic accident that nearly wiped out our family. After the accident, I spent my afternoons teaching my dad things he'd taught me ten years earlier. There was nothing so humbling, so hard, so heart-breaking, so tender.

You want to know why I'm so passionate about safety? Because it's personal. It's not a "someone else," it was me. Because I lived through the shrapnel of it. Because I know how it stings, how it hurts, how it haunts children, when the people you love are injured at work. Because there is nothing more important in this company then you, me, and us staying safe.

Standing Alone

Alice Stewart isn't a name you've probably heard of, but she has affected all of our lives. A UK physician in the early twentieth century, Alice specialized in social medicine. She keenly observed the alarming rate of cancer in children, especially babies. Epidemiological research wasn't providing any clues, so she unconventionally conducted a survey of pregnant women and new moms: moms have the answer she thought. Immediately she noticed the disparity between lower income and upper income families – those with more money had significantly higher cancer rates. Upon closer investigation, affluent families could afford x-rays of the fetus. Her results were initially regarded as unsound, but she took on the medical field. She was shunned by colleagues. Her deeper findings on fetal damage caused by x-rays of pregnant women were eventually accepted across the globe and the use of medical x-rays during pregnancy and early childhood was disapproved, although it took nearly two and a half decades.

We are faced with a leap of faith that has left this team and this company unpopular, criticized, shunned. It's been lonely and humbling. I've had my doubts as I'm sure you have...*what if we have this wrong?* But years ago, I made an equally unpopular decision and today I'm so glad I did... I believed so fervently that I was willing to take discredit. I had self-doubt, but I persisted (driven equally by ego and passion I would honestly say). I could have stopped what became a crusade for me, and no one would have blamed me nor noticed. I could have traded in for a peaceful existence, but to me shuddering my passion was no existence at all...

Prescribed Burn

Forest fires are devastating. Trees incinerated. Animals in mass migrations from their habitats. But forest fires are essential for the growth of forests. When forests reach maturity, they stagnate. The rate of detritus – dead wood – exceeds the growth of new plants, shrubs, trees. Mature forests become littered with dead matter and there is no room for new life to emerge. An entire ecosystem stagnated, on the brink of a slow death.

In some ways we are facing the same stagnation. It's not that something is wrong, just like there's nothing "wrong" with mature forests. But it's just we aren't growing, we aren't advancing with new thinking, we aren't learning faster, evolving faster. When forests reach the point beyond stagnation to decay – when decay exceeds growth in the forest then forestry experts administer prescribed burns.

We are at a crossroads – stagnation or growth. We choose growth. We need to do what we don't want – we need some prescribed burns. The growth of new forests is built right into their DNA. Seeds of the jack pine are only opened up under the intense temperatures of fire. The dead mass littering the forest floor, suffocating new seedlings in a mature forest, becomes an abundant source of nutrients for new plants, shrubs, seedlings to grow.

We need to set old practices that hold us back on fire.

We need to set complacency and excuses on fire.

We need to set rigidity on fire and let agility replace it. .

We need to set a mindset of avoid losing on fire and replace it with play to win.

I'm not suggesting that everything is broken, wrong, needs to be torched. But I am saying that we need to light some prescribed burns so we can grow again. The change will feel uncomfortable. Seeing a forest on fire, even controlled under a prescribed burn, looks horrific. But growth is on the other side.

4 HOW TO WRITE STICKY STORIES

A story isn't about the plot. Stories are about how *we change*. How we go through something difficult, an internal journey of defeat or reaching success, while we transform. Stories that move and that matter to audiences, stories that imprint and inspire, stories that pull us and nudge our emotions have a certain recipe. This doesn't mean that your essential stories won't have your fingerprints and flair. On the contrary, you'll see that as one of the essential ingredients. But scientists and storytelling sages have decoded the structure of stories that captivate. So, when you write your essential stories, you need to keep these elements in mind — the 10P's of Sticky Stories.

10 P's of Sticky Stories

Purpose. You can't begin to tell your story unless you know why it should matter to the listener. Not for you, but for them. What is the simple idea that you want impressed on them? What do you want them to recall at a moment's notice? Your stories need to have purpose, resolve, clear intent. A story isn't like striking up a conversation without knowing where it may go. Some stories seem to be pushed on us in a self-serving way. But good stories have a clear, core motivation that is about the audience, not the teller. Good stories, the stories that are told over and over again, don't need artificial drama to captivate their audiences. Your stories need to pull your audience, so they come close and listen for your wisdom from a spirit of trustworthiness.

Practical How-To: Before you start writing, contemplate, *what is my purpose for this story?* What is the single-minded essence that can be written in one sentence? What do you want the audience to think, feel, do? Listen to your heart, not just your head. What is the burning conviction deep inside you that your story is fueled from? Don't start writing until you know why your story *must* be told?

Presence. Your storytelling needs your presence and your presence is personal. Your narrative writing should not just tell your story, but express it. Your audience doesn't just want you to tell them a story; they want to feel your story. Scientists have proved that senses and emotions can have a powerful impact on memory; emotional stories are encoded in our brains and recalled more often and with more clarity than neutral events.

How do you write about your workaholism and how it almost destroyed your family? Your "never again" quality call-to-action? Your turning point as a leader when you stopped letting your fear of failure cause you to play it safe? Your joy in enlivening a mediocre employee, arousing a determination that had been buried so that he excelled? Your regret of putting profits above people? When we *feel* the *Myth-of-Origin Story* over simply telling it, we inseparably connect the founders with the listener. When we *feel* your *Who-Am-I Story* over simply telling it, it's unmistakably yours. Write your stories with the kind of passion you want listeners to feel. You want the audience to remember the details, but presence transfers more of the truth of your story.

Practical How-To: Replay the story events in your head and your heart. Give yourself permission to feel the emotions of the moment again — sweaty palms, deafening silence, clenched jaw, bitten nails, swelling pride, fist pumped. Write as if you are telling the story right there — with a chair pulled up to someone's desk, with your eyes staring intently to your team, with your arm around the shoulder of your apprentice, practically jumping up and down or crestfallen on your knees, standing tall swelling with pride. Write as if you are speaking to a team a generation from now. Write with long pauses. Repeat words and phrases for effect. For example:

This is a never again moment for us. Never again will we look the other way on a service issue. Never again will we take the easy way, the convenient way just to make a little extra money. I'm making a commit that for me never again will I...

Decide your tone and pace: a delicate whisper or practically shouting, punchy, quick-fire phrases or enunciated, deliberate sentences.

Narrate as only you can. In your voice — not too practiced, but raw. How we communicate — not the grammar or the punctuation, but the presence — matters immensely. Forget sentence structure. Get your presence across to the listener. How will they *feel* your story?

Prompts Participation. Good stories prompt voluntary participation. *Will you join me*, they beckon. They spark us to action, to raise our hands, to stand up *for*, stand up *to*, to boldly go with you. Prompting participation starts with a shared identity. When we feel like we are part of a community, then we feel connected to others in that community. We want to join. So, having your audience put themselves in your shoes, eliciting experiences that are relatable, connecting by being seen as one of them, creates the conditions for shared identity. When audiences connect, they want to join. Give us a reason to cheer for the characters.

Practical How-To: Ask, *"Have you ever been there?"* *There* isn't necessarily a place, but an emotion, a feeling, an experience that is deeply engrained in common meaning. *There* is a metaphor for something shared between the teller and the listener. You don't need to be explicit; the audience will find it themselves. For example:

> *Have you ever been there?   You know what that feels like, don't you, when…?*
>
> *Remember the first time you…?*

Small doses of humor are particularly effective at prompting participation.   Look over your story and add a little bit of humor to it. Be whimsical. Find the nuances that are amusing, eccentric, quirky, self-deprecating.

Pure Heart. Be authentic and vulnerable. If it is fake, then audiences can smell the insincerity. Don't use your story as a platform for your persona.   Don't use your story as an opportunity to validate your actions. Don't use your story as a megaphone to convince, cajole, coax in a self-serving way. Every story has a vantage point that defines the perspective, and your perspective creates a specific version to the story.   There are different vantages and therefore versions to our stories seen through contrasting angles and perspectives. The same event can be told in different ways. When we write stories, we need to understand that we write from a singular perspective that has hidden biases, assumptions, and baggage from the past. They will unconsciously creep into your story. It's not wrong, but often it's a narrow view that requires us to look in the mirror and see circumstances from other angles.

Practical How-To: Before you write, you need to cleanse your heart and mind of any hidden agendas, harbored grudges, or self-centered intentions.   Never lie. Hyperbole for effect is okay, but you may need to tell your audience that you are doing so. Re-read your story or have someone else read it looking for hidden agendas or insincerity.

Pivot. Great stories have a similar pattern.   Things were good, something awful happened, and then the protagonist fought a great battle.   There is a tension between *what is* and *what could be.*

Remember that tension fires up the attention pathway in our brain — a struggle, a test, a trying circumstance, a character flaw, a failure, a crisis, a hopeless dream. The tension spurs action. But then there's a turning point, a transition, a pivot. The music changes. So much is riding on the pivot. Not the ceasing of the crisis, not the misfortune abating, but the triumph...of becoming better, of growth prevailing..

Stories can have similar ingredients — love, loss, adventure, danger, romance, sacrifice, insurmountable odds, good vs. evil. But great stories have a pivot that leads to personal growth. Finding unusual or unknown abilities deep inside ourselves that leads to personal growth is a hardwired human motivation.

Practical How-To: Start your story planning with the pivot. The *from/to* moment, the line crossed between *what is* and *what could be*, the *but then* moment when something hung in the balance. Now look for the growth. The moment needs to mean something. What did you make of the moment?

Positivity / Placebo. Our brain doesn't know what to do with prolonged anxiety and fear. These were only meant to be activated temporarily in self-protective fight or flight. Research reveals the hidden strength of positive emotions. Positive emotions prompt brain cell growth while negative emotions prompt decay. Our brain neurons have many branches like trees. Positivity generates new branches. The longer neurons fire, the more they fire, the more intensely they fire from happiness, gratitude, hope, joy, pride, recognition, the more they are going to build pathways, branches. To hardwire happiness into the brain, our stories should lean on the positive.

When we build our legacy stories, positivity counts. Positivity releases feel-good hormones and neurotransmitters such as serotonin, dopamine, and oxytocin. Positivity makes people feel closer to one another. Positivity allows people to bounce back from life's challenges; resilience is predicted by a positivity score. Positivity is more than the absence of negativity. Dr. Barbara

Fredrickson found that people who flourish have something in common: they all experience more positivity than negativity in their everyday lives. We need to increase the quantity of positivity in our lives. That's why storytelling should have the right balance of positivity — it has fringe benefits to the listener and the teller.

Stories can alter our brain chemistry — like pumping oxytocin — and brain chemistry changes mental states and behaviors. There is a biological and psychological basis for placebos. Placebos trigger the brain to think differently which can spark the way our body behaves by flooding our body with a cornucopia of biochemicals. More than half of the impact of many medicines is due to what we believe they will achieve. Placebos can reduce blood pressure, accelerate healing, fight infections. Placebos create hope and expectations and expectations create beliefs. What do you want your audience to believe? Placebos can turn *can't do* into *can do*. Placebos can turn fear into hope.

Practical How-To: Positivity doesn't need to be at odds with a pure heart. Being authentic and real is paramount. Writing with positivity doesn't mean we have a gullible, pollyannaish approach to real tragedies or missed opportunities. But it is important to build legacy stories with an eye toward finding positive meaning in your experiences, finding gratitude for even the negative events that transformed you, finding silver linings, finding glass-half-full views.

Create placebo benefits. Exude hope that forges assurance, anticipation, an expectation so listeners believe. For example:

I know it may not seem like it today, sitting here in the circumstances we are in, but I'm telling you that this time next year...

Because we've done it before, maybe not this team, but the history of this company is built on...

Punch. When the message is clear, compelling, and simple, it's worth repeating. We need to be masters of exclusion by focusing on single-minded messages. Save sub-plots, deeper explanations, and back stories for another story. Don't be afraid to break one story into two. It's better to tell multiple stories and have them woven together as golden threads than to create a ball of yarn that can be easily tangled into a mess.

Practical How-To: Build repetition. Repetitive phrases, questions, feelings, and imagery drives remembrance but also creates a dramatic effect. Repeat "What if..." or "Just imagine..." during a *What if...Vision Story*. Repeat "I'll never forget..." during a *Defining Moment Story*.

The average person speaks about 100-150 words per minute. So if we want our stories to be about three to five minutes long, then we should be targeting 300-600 word stories. Of course, your speech or presentation might be longer, but the story should not take up the bulk of the time. This is just a rule of thumb.

Perception. Metaphors and imagery are highly sticky and memorable. The human brain has the ability to process images sixty times faster than words. Metaphors allow us to make comparisons and illuminate that which cannot be easily described in literal language. Dan and Chip Heath describe in *Made to Stick* how concrete images and sensory information propagate messaging stickiness. They provide a particularly memorable example on nutrition. When the Center for Science in the Public Interest (CPSI), a nonprofit group that educates the public about nutrition, wanted to get the public's attention on fatty foods, they didn't use scientific arguments to convince the public to reduce saturated fat intake to no more than 20 grams. They targeted a highly visible culprit – movie popcorn – which contained more than 37 grams of saturated fat and called a press conference on September 27, 1992. Here's the message it presented: "A medium-sized 'butter' popcorn at a typical neighborhood movie theater contains more artery-clogging fat than a bacon-and-eggs breakfast, a Big Mac and fries for lunch, and a steak dinner with all the trimmings — combined!" They brought visuals for the cameras to gawk over.

We think and remember in metaphors. Researchers at Emory University discovered that when subjects read an evocative metaphor rather than a simple description (e.g., the singer had a velvet voice vs. the singer had a pleasing voice; he had leathery hands vs. he had strong hands) more sensory receptors in the cortex lit up.

Practical How-To: Don't be afraid to use other's stories, imagery or metaphors. You can find great examples in history, other companies, and the natural world. These can be effective in getting complex ideas across to listeners because they are highly relatable. When you don't have what you need — borrow it. Metaphors and illustrations can be used as influence behind your ideas.

Peak End. Our memories are influenced by the intensity of the immediate experience and how it ended — a peak-end rule — according to Nobel Prize winner Daniel Kahneman. People judge an experience based on how they felt at its peak or most intense point and at its end, regardless of whether the experience is pleasant or unpleasant. Listeners will remember stories according to the peak-end rule. The duration of the experience doesn't determine the overall assessment — only the peak and the end moments matter most.

Practical How-To: When you plan your story, think about the placement of the peak and what you want them to think/feel/do at the end. Peaks often coincide with the pivot or the resolution. This is when listeners are most attentive.

Ensure your stories end where you want them to — with the lesson and the emotion. The ending and the peak are remembered most. So while we want to get listeners' attention early, don't let your ending fall flat or be easily forgotten.

Surprise. So what drives peaks? Surprise, unexpectedness, curiosity will spark our attention pathways and draw us in, sparking our immediate attention. Early in your story, you need to break patterns — the schemas or ways of thinking that we automatically anticipate — and get the audience's attention. We are creatures of habit, and we can't help but involuntarily focus on something that violates our existing schemas. Our default mode is to conserve energy and not pay attention unless it's important for our survival. Unexpectedness signals us to pay attention.

Practical How-To: Understand what your audience believes, then change their perspective. To get their attention, you need to break their mental shortcuts that lull them into dismissing the message and the messenger. Think about what blinders your audience has. Find spots to introduce unexpectedness or snippets of incomplete information that draws their curiosity

Scripting Your Stories

Collecting and curating legacy stories requires a routine. In our busy lives, taking the time to script stories isn't natural, but we can create a mindful rhythm. You need to create a habit of legacy storytelling. Social scientists have decoded how habits form. In *The Power of Habit*, Charles Duhigg decodes the synthesis of habits: motivation, ability, a trigger, and a reward.

Motivation. To write legacy stories, you need to be motivated. You need a rallying cause, an inspiration, a why. What is it about legacy story writing that is important enough to get up early on weekends or take time with a cup of coffee before starting your day?   Your motivation can be a deadline —to prepare for mentoring an apprentice, to show up for an important kick-off event or team meeting, to include in a speech at the end of a particularly difficult year, to introduce yourself to a new team.

When we make a commitment to someone else, we tend to follow through. Find a partner. When others are participating in legacy-story writing, they tend to mutually hold each other accountable. When you find someone who wants to legacy build with you, you will be more likely to follow through.

Perhaps add story crafting to the agenda during your leadership team's annual retreat or on a routine basis during staff meetings. Get in the habit of not just reporting results, but instead also telling stories.

Ability. Make the first steps easy. Mine for your stories like digging for shapeless rocks in a quarry as rough story starters. Story starters are the raw ideas, the rough concepts, the memories, the uneven experiences, the patchwork of phrases, the defining moments that you want to write about. They are jotted down notes, voice memos dictated while commuting home. They are clunky phrases and fragmented sentences scribbled on dozens of sticky notes, index cards, journal entries, napkins. Let your words be choppy, unpolished. Avoid the tendency to filter or evaluate them. You are simply collecting rocks, not choosing those to chisel into stories yet.

Inspiration for your story starters doesn't need to be highly structured. Be playful. Rummage through old performance reviews. Think about people — bosses and co-workers, customers, clients and suppliers. Think about proud achievements and intense mistakes. Your memories will come back. Pay attention to the feelings that flood you. Notice how your pulse changes or why you figuratively (or physically) shake your head. Pay attention to the words you say silently to yourself. They are distinctive marks for your story starters.

Find similarities. What legends, movies or story characters feel like your own story or epitomize your story? Why? What does that say about you? Why do you relate to this story? What stories impressed you as a child or impress you now as an adult? How does this remind you or something from your experience?

Write a legacy statement. When you think about transitioning from company to company, from one division to the next or when you decide to leave the workforce altogether — what do you want said about you? I want to be remembered distinctly and above all else for _____

Create a story journal or write story starters on index cards with a rough outline below:

Headline: Try to write the headline for your story that is dramatic, emotional, gripping, suspenseful, curiosity-creating.

Example: *Addiction took everything from me.*

Purpose: Why must this story be told? What difference do you want this story to make?

Example: *Disadvantaged starting point as a youth forged a drive for redemption, for a different ending to the predictable story of lost.*

Beginning: What is the tension or what is in conflict?

Example: *Broken home from alcohol and drugs. Vacillating between anger and withdrawal. Expectations for self were capped by the circumstances around me. I was always negative and hopeless. I always carried around a figurative umbrella because I expected rain in my life.*

Middle: What is the resolution to the tension, the climax?

Example: *Turning point was a co-worker telling me that my life was partly to mostly sunny, not always cloudy — that change in perception changed everything. I set high standards for myself. Positivity and hope became my hallmark. People would anticipate my quotes of the day.*☺

End: What is the lesson and emotional meaning you want to get across?

Example: *Life can be self-fulfilling. People along the way can be catalysts. Change in perception and attitude can literally change your life. From a dead-end crack kid who'd given-up before he even started anything to a courageous leader who mentors dozens of adults and kids with an always sunny smile.*

Your Trigger. You need a trigger, a reminder for legacy writing. Find the margin to write. What time and place allows you to think freely while also establishing a repetitive routine? Routine is vital, so start with a definitive goal (e.g., one story on the first Sunday of every month with a cup of coffee and a biscotti). You need to put story-writing on your calendar, set a reminder on your phone, write it on your refrigerator, or substitute it with another routine. When can you decompress and reflect? Is there a day of the week or a time of day that you can commit to? Maybe you set aside fifteen minutes every month at a staff meeting to share legacy stories. Set a time and a place and stick to the routine.

Reward yourself. The adherence to a routine is important for habit formation, but you also need a reward. The reward is happiness hormones. The happiness hormones — endorphins, serotonin, oxytocin and dopamine — flood your body when you feel proud, accomplished, connected. Your body craves them and they are the encouragement (and reminder) to "repeat" when we experience something good.

Plan when you will share your stories. Savor the feedback. I once told a story, and after, a listener told a colleague, "When he told that story, I left that meeting with the confidence to attack a mammoth." Few things can boost the confidence of the storyteller more.

5 WHAT STORY WILL YOU TELL?

There's one more story you need to tell.
It is the most important story.
It's the story you tell yourself.

What do you believe about yourself?   Your goodness, your greatness, your strengths?   Is this all, or are you made for more?

What do you tell yourself when you fall? Not _____ enough or next time?

What do you tell yourself when you nail it, achieve the impossible, overcome the insurmountable? Lucky or gritty?

What do you tell yourself when the odds are stacked against you, when the storms come rolling in, when darkness closes in? Am I doomed, or it's my finest hour?

What do you tell yourself about your position, place in the organization chart, contribution to the team? Am I at the bottom of the pile, or am I essential?

Will the chapters of your story — a derailed career path, a betrayal, a detour — define you or redeem you? Will you carry it around like old baggage or pick yourself up with a few banged up bruises?

What will you leave behind that out-survives you? Nothing much or something enduring, remarkable, and generous?

The story you tell yourself needs to be — must be — positive and encouraging, hopeful and proud, authentic, real, legacy-worthy. The story you tell yourself must be a hero's journey, an epic journey marked by moments of triumph and moments of defeat that ultimately transform the people you touch, the initiatives that touch you, the causes you carry. Whoever you are today, don't put the period there. There's more to the story; there's more to every story.

We all dream of being legendary, but there is a false notion that heroism is a scarce commodity. You don't need to slay dragons to be a hero. You don't need to be a super-hero, but a super human being who uses what she or he has for other people. You are more heroic than you think you are. Beating cancer is heroic. Cancelling a product launch because the quality just wasn't good enough is heroic. Never missing your kids' games is heroic. Speaking when no one else will is heroic. Giving someone a second chance is heroic. Generosity is heroic. Serving others is heroic. Mentoring others is heroic. Kindness is heroic. Breaking paradigms is heroic. Vulnerability is heroic. Taking a stand is heroic.

We may not start our day doing something epic, but we could end up there — fully present throughout the day, recognizing that there is the potential to make everyday moments uncommon.

Legacy leadership is a choice. Apprenticing, boldness, connection, culture — these are choices. You might choose to be the initiator, the amplifier, the encourager, the person who puts her hand up first, the person who stands not sits. You might choose to be selfless and proactive — putting in more than you take out, surprising everyone with a seemingly endless wellspring of generosity. You might be the catalyst for change, a spark that swells a revolution. Or you might be a bystander, a naysayer, a doubter, an energy vampire, a cynic, a critic, someone who never offers a solution but is quick to show what's wrong. You might choose to build up others, help them become better, maybe even until they eclipse you. Or you can worry about the individual prominence you have achieved. You can choose either path. They both create legacy — either positive legacy or negative legacy — the brunt of jokes or the talk around conference rooms and kitchen tables alike. Legacyful or legacyless. Legacy sweet or bitter. Remembered or forgotten. Intentional or accidental. Lasting or temporary. Positive or negative. Meaningful or meaningless.

You have hundreds of perfectly legitimate reasons why you should just sit and wait.

Waiting for someone to go first.

Waiting for someone to tell you what to do.

Waiting for someone to lead you.

Waiting for just the right time when you aren't so busy.

But what if, everyone else is just waiting too.

Remember that your legacy isn't being built when you want it to be or when you're ready to pay attention to it. Your legacy is always being built. Always imprinting. Always projecting. Small choices everyday add up. The things we do when we think no one is watching, this is how people will measure us. Even though nobody might notice, you know in your gut that what you're doing matters. So, write the stories you want to be told. Create legacy moments. Seize the moments that occur in the blink of an eye. Don't let them pass without you putting your fingerprints on them. You can create a culture which defines the path of your team. You can create apprentices that can eventually become master builders. You can engender a spirit of boldness to shape your category, your industry, your company. You can connect to people in ways that inspire them and give them belonging. Whether you are early in your career or a few years from retirement, make the moments count. People can and will get dozens of good-enough bosses and leaders, but you will mark them differently.

If you lead from the heart.

If you are in business to make people's lives better.

If you will lean in when others hold back.

If you are the one who is the spark, who initiates projects, who fosters hope, who generously gives more than she takes, who brings a can-do attitude despite the circumstances.

If people are your inspiration.

If you want to build something meaningful, not an empire.

If you will create a culture that brings out the best in your teammates individually, collectively.

If you honor the monumental, once-in-a-lifetime privilege of leading others.

If you make a lasting imprint in the organization.

If you shun shortcuts and want more than quick wins and quick bucks.

If you believe your stories aren't just meant for you, but for many.

If you start each day with the intention of being missed tomorrow.

Then you will build legacy.

A leader's job is to motivate people, and we motivate people by engaging their hearts. The key to their hearts is story. So ask: what story do I want to tell?

The missing link in leadership is growing our employees to become leaders. Leaders aren't born, they are made. So ask: what are your "made" stories?

Legacy leaders meticulously shape stories that are memorable, compelling, and worth repeating. They warm us on the inside. They ignite us to action. They capture our imagination. They grab our attention. They move us emotionally. They get us up on our feet. They break our paradigms and teach us. They cause our hearts to race. They are easily recalled when we are staring at difficult choices. They get us moving. They give us hope. They are told not just once, but picked up over and over again. Stories are the stones on which a legacy foundation is built. You have been investing years, decades, in the unseen quarry of stories. Ordinary pieces of everyday rock are buried beneath our busy schedules – wonderful bits of wisdom. Legacy is transferred through stories, secured through stories, cemented through stories.

When you tell a story about failure, you imprint taking risks and accept less than perfect outcomes.

When you tell a story about accountability, your imprint delivering results not simply checking the boxes.

When you tell a story about owning mistakes, you imprint raw honesty and trustworthiness.

When you tell a story about gratitude, you imprint appreciation and humility.

When you tell a story about overcoming fear amid against-the-odds circumstances, you imprint tenacity, bravery and resilience.

When you tell a story about standing alone when your values were on the line, you imprint fortitude and uncompromising character.

What story do you want to tell? The best stories, those that capture our attention and imagination, those that stay with us for a while…those are the stories of resilience amid devastation, stories of abundance amid smallness, stories of personal transformation amid devastating setbacks, stories of comebacks. Then there are those stories that re-direct our own stories. Stories when someone took a chance on you. Stories of someone believing in you even when you didn't. Stories of someone re-labelling you, seeing something in you, removing your self-doubt, revealing out your hidden talents, bringing out the best in you. Listen to your own story. Connect the dots. See the patterns and the breathtaking scenes. Your story has unique characters, surprising plot twists, and life-altering themes. There is tension and suspense, tragedy and redemption, surpassing joy and deep embraces, tearful goodbyes and heart-pounding starts, awe-stricken spiritual moments, and wide-eyed beginnings.

A company, a team, an organization without a story is a

company, a team, an organization without a purpose. A company, a team, an organization without stories is lost.

Wherever the foundation of your business, focus there and dig for the story stones. This is the place people want to gather. They come to hear the mythic stories. Draw on all those stories that have stirred your soul, flooded you with pride, stirred up the insurgent, the revolutionary, the torchbearer in you. You will need them all.

Let's end where we began.

We all want to be known for something; we all have adjectives in mind. What do you really want to be known for?

Who, when they look back, will say that you are one of the greatest leaders they have worked for?

Who will be better because of you?

What will you leave behind? Will it be lasting? Will it be inspiring? Will it matter?

We all leave something behind.

Will it out-survive you? Will it make a difference— however great or small — to your co-workers, to your team, to your company? Are you leaving your unique "fingerprints on the clay" not for your sake, but for theirs?

What stories do you want to be passed on to those around you, behind you, in front of you?

You are poised to leave a lasting legacy, a well for thirsty souls, a compass for the lost. But you need to believe that you have that potential to be a master builder, a torchbearer, a culture cultivator, a legacy statesman. You need to apprentice, to connect, to be bold and to create a leadership culture. You need to believe that you have a remarkable story to tell. Your best chapters haven't been written yet. You aren't ready for the epilogue yet. The world wants to — needs to — hear your stories.

Works Cited

Aaker, David and Jennifer. (2016). *What are Your Signature Stories?* Stanford Graduate School of Business Working Paper #3391.

Abrams, Allison. How a Toxic Work Environment Affects Your Mental Health. www.verywellmind.com. May 23, 2018.

Andrea L. Barrocas, M. (2012 Jul). Rates of Nonsuicidal Self-Injury in Youth: Age, Sex, and Behavioral Methods in a Community Sample. *Pediatrics*, 39-45.

Bariso, Justin. It Took Jeff Bezos Exactly 5 Words to Teach a Major Lesson in Emotional Intelligence. www.inc.com. 10/9/2018.

Beard, Alison and Nicholas McGinn podcast. Toxic Workplaces transcript. *Harvard Business Review*. May 3, 2018.

Brandenburger, Adam. Inside Intel. *Harvard Business Review*. N/D 1996.

Brickman, Chris. (2014) *The Brilliance of Failure*. Archway Publishing.

Cameron, Tim. *The Forty-Day Word Fast*. (2015)

Chowdhury, Subir. *The Difference*. (2017). Crown Business.

Clemmer, J. (1999). *Growing the Distance*.

Collins, Jim. (2001). *Good to Great*. Harper Business.

Delgado, J. (2018). *Negativity is Contagious*. Retrieved from psychology-spot.com: https://psychology-spot.com/positive-thinking-negative-people/

Doborovski, Katina. The Story of Chobani is about much more than yogurt. *www.medium.com*. April 28, 2017.

Duarte, Nancy and Sanchez, Patti. *(2016). Illuminate*. Penguin.

Fast Company. Chobani Founder says he simply started. January 27, 2017.

Fifth Ring, A Beautiful Constraint, May 18, 2015, https://blog.fifthring.com/a-beautiful-constraint

Godin, Seth. *What to Do When It's Your Turn*. (2014)

Green House Project White Paper, Green House Project web site (2018) www.greenhouseproject.org/resources/research

Hetrick, R. (2018, August 27). How I Built This With Guy Raz. (G. R. NPR, Interviewer)

Make-A-Wish: How It All Started: Chris' Wish. www.wish.org.

Morgan, A. (2015) *A Beautiful Constraint*. Wiley.

National Public Radio, *How to build a better job*, March 29, 2016. *Hidden Brain newscast*

Perkins, Dennis. *Leading at the Edge: Leadership Lessons from the Extraordinary Saga of Shakleton's Antarctic Expedition*. Amcom, 2000.

Richter, Curt P. (1957). On the phenomenon of sudden death in animals and man. *Psychosom. Med.*, 19, 191-8

Schein, E. (2016). *Organizational Culture and Leadership, 5th ed.* Jossey-Bass.

Sherrie Bourg Carter, P. (2012, Oct 20). *Emotions are Contagious - Choose Your Company Wisely.* Retrieved from *Psychology Today.*

Stillman, Jessica. Your Co-Workers' Bad Attitudes Are Contagious, Study Says. www.cbsnews.com, Jan 21, 2011.

Survey, E. A. (2018).

Sutton, R. (2017). Memo to CEO: Are you the source of workplace dysfunction? *McKinsey Quarterly*.

Tedlow, Richard. Intel: The Education of Any Grove. *Fortune*. March 22, 2016.

Tough, Paul. (2012). *How Children Succeed.* Houghton Mifflin Harcourt.

Useem, Michael. (1998). *The Leadership Moment.* Random House.

Watkinson, Jim. *Walt Disney's Grit*. www.innovationat work.wordpress.com, 8/8/2018.

CREATE *your* STORY

LEAVING LEGACY

ABOUT THE AUTHOR

Bruce Williamson is the author of *Marked in Stone: Building Your Family Legacy*. He has been a senior leader across numerous award-winning marketing and innovation teams in the consumer packaged goods and healthcare industries. He was the co-founder of a nutrition start-up company and has served on the board of several nonprofits. He holds an MBA from the University of Michigan Ross School of Business and a BS in Engineering from University of Wisconsin-Madison.

Made in the USA
Middletown, DE
09 December 2018